Michael Haykin with Ron Baines

DayOne

Series Editor: Brian H Edwards

DayOne

TRAVEL
WITH

Jonathan Edwards, A God-centered life, an enduring legacy

23

2 Pursuing the glory of God

Jonathan Edwards' Puritan heritage revealed itself in his seventy resolutions resolves to live passionately, and with every breath, for the glory of God. These resolutions set the tone for much of his life and ministry to come

IN August of 1722, the young Jonathan Edwards, not yet 19 years old, made the journey to New York City to take up pastoral responsibilities in a small Presbyterian congregation. While he was serving this congregation, it occupied a building on William Street between Wall Street and Liberty Street (then Little Queen Street) in now Lower Manhattan

Above: The port of New York in the eighteenth century

Facing page: The present Meeting House in the First Church of New Haven. During Jonathan Edwards' day, it would have stood with the First Church as it would James Pierpont, his fellow minister and son-in-law to pastor

---

46

Esther Edwards Burr and her diary

Reading Esther's diary reveals that one of the things she prized was spiritual friendship with women like Sarah Prince. Writing on 20 April 1758, she reminisces she told Sarah, "...highly value...friends than one might anticipate.

Below and inset: The Dwight family plot in Bridge Street's cemetery, Northampton. The inscription on the Edwards family tombstones. The Dwight family beginning with Mary Edwards Dwight and husband Timothy

47

Right: The grave of Timothy and Mary Edwards Dwight in the Bridge Street cemetery in Northampton, Massachusetts.

Left: The grave of Timothy Dwight in Grove Street cemetery, New Haven, CT. The inscription damaged and worn.

CONTENTS

© Day One Publications 2013 First printed 2013

A CIP record is held at The British Library   ISBN 978-1-84625-390-4

published by Day One Publications Ryelands Road, Leominster, HR6 8NZ

01568 613 740 FAX 01568 611 473 email: sales@dayone.co.uk www.dayone.co.uk All rights reserved

gn: Kathryn Chedgzoy Printed by Polskabook, UK

cation: To my 'dear companion' Alison Elizabeth Haykin & to Ellen Joan Baines, a 'daughter of Abraham'
a descendant of Sarah and Jonathan, and that dearest of gifts these past 32 years.

Meet Jonathan Edwards

Born in the wilds of America, on the very edge of the British Empire, his books and thought revolutionized his world, and today he is recognized as the leading theologian of the eighteenth century.

Jonathan Edwards grew up with his ten sisters in a pastor's home in central Connecticut. Heir to the spiritual riches of the Puritans, he did not hesitate to reshape aspects of that heritage so that it could speak powerfully to the men and women of his day. His beautiful wife Sarah played a key role in enabling him to accomplish all that he did.

Edwards' longest pastorate was at Northampton, Massachusetts, where he and his congregation went through two significant spiritual revivals. He defended these revivals—though not without some criticism of them—in a series of books, of which the most important is The *Religious Affections*. Sadly, there were some in his church who deeply resented his theology, and in 1750 they were instrumental in his dismissal.

Edwards was offered a college presidency in Scotland, but family considerations won, and he became pastor of a church on the wild frontier at Stockbridge. Here, in the early stages of the French and Indian War, he faithfully shepherded his flock which mostly consisted of Indians.

In 1757 Edwards reluctantly accepted the offer of the presidency of the College of New Jersey, but he died shortly after taking office in 1758.

Fundamental to his life was an unquenchable passion for the honour of God's glory and a fascination with God's beauty. For modern-day Christians, who often seem unaware of both, the story of Jonathan Edwards is indispensable.

Jonathan Edwards

Facing Page: Portraits of Jonathan and Sarah in the Maclean House, Princeton University, New Jersey

❶ Jonathan's 'inward, sweet delight in God'

Raised in a Puritan home, Jonathan Edwards had deep doubts about God's sovereignty yet became one of its greatest champions; he was a shy boy who would stand before large congregations as a spokesman for God

When the Puritan preacher Thomas Hooker left England because of religious persecution, he settled for a short time in the Netherlands before ultimately setting sail for Massachusetts in 1633. Sailing with Hooker was another influential Puritan leader, John Cotton. Hooker had been invited to the Massachusetts Bay Colony by the church in Newtown (now Cambridge) where he settled upon arrival in the Bay Colony, rejoining some of his parishioners who had preceded him from England.

The Old Parish (as it is now called) was to be a significant work in New England

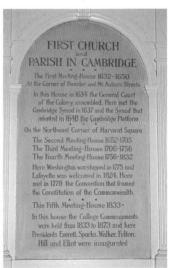

Above left: Ministers of the First Church in Cambridge, Massachusetts

Above right: Plaque opposite Ministers list

Facing page: First Church, Northampton; this is a successor to the building Jonathan Edwards would have known and was built in 1833 (see page 49)

Left: Founders Monument, Hartford, CT. Included on this monument are the names of James Cole (who married the widow of Richard Edwards, Jonathan's great-great-grandmother), as well as William Edwards, Jonathan's great-grandfather

Congregational history. Under Hooker's successor, Thomas Shepherd, this church would see the establishment in 1648 of the Cambridge Platform, which became the standard for church government in much of New England; the church also founded the first college in the colony in 1636, soon named after a significant benefactor, Rev. John Harvard. In 1637 it was also the scene of the trial of Anne Hutchinson who was accused of being an antinomian (someone who denies the importance of

God's moral law). However, by the time most of these things transpired, Thomas Hooker and the majority of the church in Newtown had relocated westward to the banks of the Connecticut River where they established a small frontier settlement known as Hartford.

Timothy Edwards and his children

Among those who travelled with Hooker was a young man of around eighteen years named William Edwards. His father, Richard Edwards, had been a minister in London but had died sometime earlier. William Edwards settled in Hartford, where he married and had a son, Richard, born in 1647; Richard was the first of the Edwards line born on American soil. Later in life Richard became a prosperous merchant in Hartford. Sadly, his marriage was anything but prosperous. Soon after his marriage to Elizabeth Tuttle in 1667, she admitted to being pregnant by another man. Richard was willing to overlook this, but it soon became apparent that the woman was afflicted with a profound mental illness, and over the next twenty-four years, after repeated infidelities along with outbreaks of anger and threats of violence against her husband, he was granted a divorce—something almost unheard of in Puritan New England. Timothy Edwards, Jonathan's father, was born to them in 1669.

Timothy was educated at Harvard, then under the presidency of Increase Mather, where he was not only taught by some of the best thinkers of the day, but also where he was exposed to some of the most prominent preachers, including Increase's son, Cotton Mather. Timothy received both his BA and his MA from Harvard and from there took up teaching to earn his living. It was while Timothy was teaching in Northampton, Massachusetts, that he received a call to become the first pastor of the newly established Second Church of Windsor, Connecticut.

Windsor had been founded in 1633 at the junction of the Farmington and Connecticut rivers; it was originally named Dorchester (the Indians called it

Understanding Puritanism

The word 'Puritan' first appeared in the English language in the early 1560s. It was originally used as a term of reproach to designate those who wished to reform or 'purify' the Church of England according to the Scriptures. The Puritans were first and foremost a Bible-centred people. The monarch at the time of the emergence of Puritanism was Elizabeth I who reigned from 1559 to 1603. She was content with a church that, though fully Protestant in theology, was also one in which the queen functioned as the head of the Church and in which the worship still retained much from the medieval Roman Catholic Church. The Puritan movement arose as a direct response to this, and it sought to bring about a complete reformation, in worship and church government as well as in doctrine.

Until the 1620s, the Puritans and their Anglican opponents largely agreed on how a person becomes a Christian. In this decade however, King Charles I who reigned from 1625 to1649, began to appoint to high positions in the Church of England men who emphasized the decisive role that the human will plays in salvation. This theological position, known as Arminianism after its Dutch founder Jacob Arminius (1560–1609), was seen by the Puritans as nothing less than a betrayal of the Reformation heritage which was unequivocal in its proclamation of the sovereignty of God in salvation. Puritanism thus came to stand for loyalty to the Reformation's view of salvation.

Above all, the Puritans were primarily men and women intensely passionate about piety and Christian experience. The Elizabethan Puritan leader, William Perkins, put it well when he said that the Puritans were 'those that most endeavour to get and keep purity of heart'. See also 'The Puritans and the Civil War' in *Travel with John Bunyan* in this series pp 14–15.

Above: The graves of Richard Edwards (left) and his second wife Mary in the Ancient Burying Ground Hartford, CT

Below: Statue of John Harvard Cambridge, MA

Matianuck). The lands east of the river were ideal for raising crops such as rye and Indian corn, and by 1691 there were approximately fifty families living there with some three hundred people able to attend church.

However, crossing the Connecticut River by ferry could be precarious, especially with winter ice and spring floods. Consequently a decision was made to establish a second meeting house in Windsor on the eastern bank of the river. Timothy Edwards was called as the first minister of this new church in November 1694, along with his new bride, Esther Stoddard, the daughter of the famed Solomon Stoddard of Northampton, Massachusetts. Timothy and Esther would have eleven children in this farming community (originally called Windsor Farms but now known as East Windsor)—ten daughters and one son. After the birth

Right: Bissel Ferry
plaque, East Windsor,
CT

Below: Bissel Ferry site
from the East Windsor
side of the Connecticut
River

of four daughters,
their son Jonathan
was born 5 October
1703. Six more sisters
would follow between
the years 1705 and
1718. In a day of high
mortality rates, it is
amazing that all of
these children grew
to adulthood. Also
remarkable in a day
when shorter statures
were the norm, was
the fact that Jonathan
and his sisters were
all at least six feet tall
and Timothy cracked
jokes about his 'sixty
feet of daughters'!

It was here in
East Windsor that
Timothy Edwards
faithfully served as
a minister of the gospel until his
death in 1758, some sixty-four
years after his coming to the area.
He also took pains to educate
not only Jonathan, but also his
daughters. Excellent insight into
this colonial home-school can be
found in a letter Timothy wrote
to his wife Esther in 1711, when
he had been enlisted as a chaplain
in the British army in the fight
against the French and Indians

during what was known as
Queen Anne's War (1703–1713).
Timothy told his wife: 'I desire
thee to take care that Jonathan
don't loose what he hath learned.'
Since Jonathan's four older sisters
were helping in tutoring their
brother, their father had some
advice regarding their studies as
well: 'I would also have the girls
keep what they have learnt of the
grammar, and get by heart as far

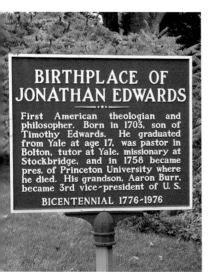

Top left: *Jonathan Edwards' birth marker at East Windsor, CT*

Below left and inset: *God's Acre Cemetery East Windsor, CT*

Right: *Timothy Edwards' plaque at the entrance to God's Acre Cemetery*

as Jonathan hath learnt. He can help them to read as far as he hath learnt: and [I] would have both him and them keep their writing, and therefore write much oftener than they did when I was at home. I have left paper enough for them which they may use to the end, only I would have you reserve enough for your own use in writing letters.'

Jonathan's ten sisters

In addition to giving his daughters an education similar to that of his son, Timothy sent all but one of his daughters to a finishing school in Boston. This education produced strong, spiritually-focused women, who were not afraid to speak their minds. One of the girls, Jerusha, who died at nineteen in 1729 and after whom Jonathan's more famous daughter was named, was known for taking long walks for meditation in the woods near East Windsor and for reading Scripture well into the night. Another, Hannah, who did not marry until she was thirty-three, maintained that singleness

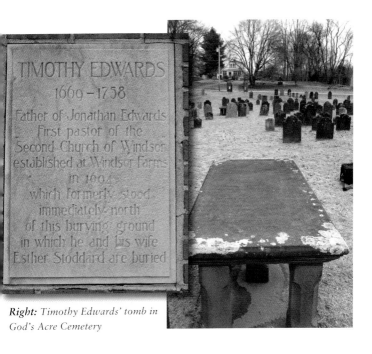

Right: *Timothy Edwards' tomb in God's Acre Cemetery*

can be a blessing to women 'if they can make religion and knowledge their chief end.'

During the time of spiritual revival known as the Great Awakening (1740–1742), in which, as we shall see, Jonathan Edwards played a key role, his eldest sister Esther was firmly opposed to the revival. In her Diary entry for August 1743 she noted, 'I was last night in company with one of the "New Lights" [that is, one in favour of the revival]. I could hardly bear the room.' Nor did she keep her views to herself and to her Diary. The following March, she made known her problems with the revival to her brother, and they had a strong disagreement about the awakening. Again she wrote in her Diary: 'Some things occurred this morning which made it

appear very doubtful whether my dear brother would ever come off of some principles which appeared to me were detrimental to religion.'

One of the most humorous incidents associated with the Edwards family concerns yet another sister Martha, the youngest of them. It seems she had a strong temper, and when she was being courted by a certain minister, Timothy warned the prospective son-in-law that his youngest daughter was not at all easy to live with. The man, though, was not lightly put off and he continued to press his suit by emphasizing that he had heard Martha was the recipient of saving grace. 'Oh yes,' the father responded, 'Martha is a good girl, but…the grace of God will dwell where you or I cannot!'

Top: The gravestone of Jonathan Edwards' sister Jerusha, in God's Acre Cemetery

Above: The grave of Jonathan's mother, Esther, in God's Acre Cemetery

Jonathan's early religious experience

It was in this East Windsor farming community that the young Jonathan experienced his first spiritual affections. He had certainly been no stranger to spiritual awakening, for there had been examples of this in the lives of other members of his father's congregation. He records the first of a number of significant spiritual events in his life in what is known as the *Personal Narrative*. He refers to a time when there was a remarkable spiritual awakening in his father's congregation. Jonathan mentions how he was deeply affected for many months: 'Concerned about the things of religion, and my soul's salvation; and was abundant in religious duties.' According to Edwards' own record, he 'used to pray five times a day in secret, and to spend much time in religious conversation with other boys; and used to meet with them to pray together.'

In fact, he and a number of these friends built what Edwards called 'a booth in a swamp, in a very retired spot, for a place of prayer'. There were also occasions, Edwards records, when he would spend time by himself praying in 'secret places of my own in the woods'. These were times of deep emotional impact. 'My affections,' Edwards writes in his *Personal Narrative*, 'seemed to be lively and easily moved, and I

Right: The grave of Jonathan Edwards' sister Esther Hopkins in West Springfield, MA

Below: This house, standing beside God's Acre Cemetery in East Windsor, was the home of Asahel Nettleton, Calvinistic preacher during the Second Great Awakening, and one of the founders of the Theological Seminary originally located in East Windsor. His grave, as well as that of his biographer Bennet Tyler, is located in the cemetery behind the Ellsworth School across from the old seminary's President's House in East Windsor

seemed to be in my element when engaged in religious duties. And I am ready to think, many are deceived with such affections, and such a kind of delight as I then had in religion, and mistake it for grace.' However, Edwards went on to confess that soon his 'convictions and affections wore off; and I entirely lost all those affections and delights, and left

off secret prayer, at least as to any constant performance of it.'

Studying at Yale and conversion

Jonathan left East Windsor to attend college in September of 1716 when he was just short of his thirteenth birthday. Since Harvard was evidencing signs of departure from the old ways

of Puritan orthodoxy, it had been decided that Jonathan was to be educated at the fledgling Collegiate School of Connecticut which had been founded in 1701. The Collegiate School of Connecticut was based in two towns at this time, Killingworth and Saybrook, both of them hoping to become the permanent locale for the college. By the time Jonathan was ready to enter college, the school had yet a third branch in Wethersfield, Connecticut, where one of Edwards' cousins, Elisha Williams, was the main teacher. The school would eventually consolidate its campuses in 1718 and settle in New Haven, taking the name of a generous benefactor, Elihu Yale. It was from this campus that Jonathan

Edwards received his BA in 1720. He graduated top in his class and was chosen to give the valedictory address—which would have been in Latin. However, his education was not finished, and he decided to continue his studies and returned the following school year to begin pursuing an MA.

In the summer of 1721 Jonathan had an experience in which there was lasting evidence that the young man had now been genuinely converted to Christ. He describes the event in his *Personal Narrative*. He first emphasized that from his childhood onwards his mind had been filled with a deep hatred of 'the doctrine of God's sovereignty, in choosing whom he would to eternal life, and rejecting whom he pleased;

Below and inset: Theological Seminary President's House, East Windsor

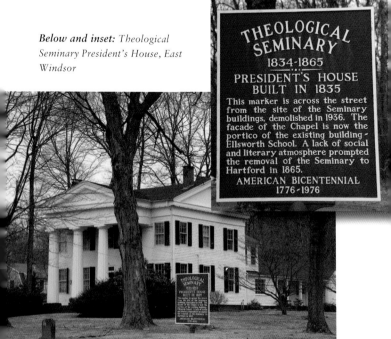

Right: The grave of Elisha Williams in Old Wethersfield, CT

leaving them eternally to perish, and be everlastingly tormented in hell.' Edwards said that he considered this doctrine to be an utterly 'horrible' belief. However, there came a time when he was 'convinced, and fully satisfied, as to this sovereignty of God, and his justice in thus eternally disposing of men, according to his sovereign pleasure.' Since then, Edwards noted, the sovereignty of God in salvation 'has very often appeared exceeding pleasant, bright, and sweet.'

Jonathan knew roughly when it was that he experienced this 'sort of inward, sweet delight in God and divine things.' He was reading the apostle Paul's words in 1 Timothy 1:17, 'Now unto the King, eternal, immortal, invisible, the only wise God, be honour and glory forever and ever, Amen.' As he pondered over these words,

> 'There came into my soul, and was as it were diffused through it, a sense of the glory of the Divine Being; a new sense, quite different from anything I ever experienced before. Never any words of Scripture seemed to me as these words did. I thought with myself, how excellent a Being that was, and how happy I should be, if I might enjoy that God, and be rapt [i.e. taken away] up to him in heaven; and be as it were swallowed up in him forever!'

Not surprisingly, Edwards would later remark that the conversion of a human being is as great a work of God as the creation of the entire universe. The young graduate student had gained what no earthly education could give him, a settled assurance and lasting joy of the knowledge of God found in Christ.

Jonathan completed his graduate studies in May of 1722, thus giving him the academic grounding that would be foundational to his becoming '*the* theologian of revival', as the twentieth-century Welsh preacher D. Martyn Lloyd-Jones loved to describe him. But there were two other aspects of his preparation that were yet in need of maturing. If he was to spend the better part of the next four decades in the pulpit and as a pastor he needed to mature in these areas as well.

An event in the autumn following the completion of his graduate studies also set the tone for aspects of his later ministry.

Left: *Old North Church, Boston*

imprisoned and fined because they refused to be bound by the strictures of Anglican worship. And now, in the very heartland of the Puritan world in New England, Yale College, the flag of the persecutor had been unfurled. Little wonder that this incident became known as the 'Connecticut apostasy'! Cutler subsequently left Yale and travelled to England for what he deemed to be a proper ordination in the Church of England. He returned to Boston settling at Christ Church (now known as the Old North Church) where he remained for the rest of his life, faithful to Anglicanism. To the young college this was a great trial.

At the commencement exercises of Yale College in September of 1722, those assembled for this auspicious occasion were utterly shocked to hear the respected Rector of Yale College, Timothy Cutler (see picture on page 112), use at the conclusion of his prayer, a well-known expression from the Anglican Book of Common Prayer: 'And let all the people say, Amen'. It might seem a small point today, but recall: the forebears of the Congregationalists in New England had been forced to leave old England because of persecution by the Anglican state. Their great-grandparents and grandparents had been

Edwards had studied with Cutler and had deeply admired the man and his learning. However, when Edwards was asked to give the address at the Yale commencement in the autumn of 1723, he made sure that his words revealed his love of, and stalwart commitment to, New England orthodoxy. A love of correct doctrine would henceforth mark all of Edwards' writing and preaching.

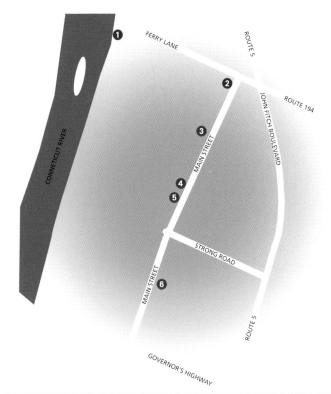

EAST WINDSOR, CT

1 BISSELL FERRY
2 OLD POST OFFICE
3 ELLSWORTH SCHOOL AND
  ASAHEL NETTLETON'S GRAVE

4 GOD'S ACRE CEMETERY
5 ASAHEL NETTLETON'S HOME
6 PLAQUE OF EDWARDS' BIRTHSITE

TRAVEL INFORMATION

Note that most web addresses in these Travel Guides are no longer included as they are easily located through any web search engine.

Hartford—The Old Statehouse

Old State House, 800 Main Street, Hartford, CT 06103 ☎ 860–522–6766.

Built in 1796 and renovated in 1996, a storehouse of information on the founding of Hartford and the Colony of Connecticut. In addition to the general historical information that can be found there, it boasts the famous bronze statue of Thomas Hooker sculpted by Frances L. Wadsworth.

The Ancient Burying Ground of Hartford Connecticut is located only a few blocks south of the Old State House and adjacent to the Center Church at the corner of Gold and Main Streets. It is here that Thomas Hooker and Samuel Stone are buried. Admission is free. The gates are open May 1—Oct. 31, 10 a.m. to 4 p.m. Mon-Sat. A fine brochure called A Walking Tour of the Ancient Burying Ground of Hartford, Connecticut is available from the Old State House. ☎ 860–228–1517 or 860–522–0855. Additional information is available through the Hartford Guides at ☎ 860–522–0855.

East Windsor Hill (Windsor Farms)

The early history of East Windsor Hill is wrapped up with the history of Windsor, CT (Connecticut's oldest English community which was settled in 1633 and incorporated in 1636) and South Windsor, CT. East Windsor did not become a separate town until 1768 and the southern half of that town, in which Windsor Farms is situated, did not become a separate community until 1845.

Windsor's Historical Society is nestled in the heart of the town center.

96 Palisado Avenue, Windsor, CT 06095. ☎ 860–688–3813.

The staff are well informed and helpful. A fine street map of Windsor and further area visitor information can be obtained through the Windsor Connecticut Tourist Information Center, 261 Broad St , Windsor, CT. ☎ 860–688–5165, or by visiting their website.

Old Wethersfield, CT

Wethersfield is one of the early homes of the Collegiate School of Connecticut (now Yale). Edwards studied under the tutelage of his cousin Elisha Williams at Wethersfield from 1716 to 1719 at which time the students removed to New Haven, the settled location for the school. The buildings used for the school during these years are no longer standing. However, the Buttolph-Williams House still stands and has become a museum. Additionally, Elisha Williams' grave is to be found in the Ancient Burying Ground directly behind the First Church of Christ, the congregation with whom Edwards worshiped during his collegiate years here. The original building is no longer standing but the current building, (constructed in 1764) is a magnificent example of 18th century church architecture.

Old Wethersfield is located just south of Hartford and is rich with colonial Connecticut history and has numerous homes, museums and gardens available to the public. A wealth of information is also available at the Historical Society's website.

Left: *The Buttolph-Williams House in Wethersfield built in 1711; a home that Williams and Edwards would have been familiar with. Williams was Jonathan's teacher as a student at Yale and his cousin*

Wethersfield Historical Society

150 Main Street, Wethersfield, CT 06109
☎ 860–529–7656.

A Visitor's Center and Museum Shop are also available.

Wethersfield Museum at Keeney Memorial (including the Wethersfield Visitor's Center)

200 Main St, Wethersfield, CT

First Church of Christ

250 Main Street, Wethersfield, CT 06109, 860–529–1575.

The current structure of the First Church dates to 1764 and, due to its restoration, is a wonderful example of mid-eighteenth century church architecture. The meeting house still exhibits the original pulpit and houses a replica of Jonathan Edwards' reading desk. The facility is generally open 9–5 Mon-Fri. and on Sunday for worship. Individuals are welcome. Occasional group tours are scheduled through the Historical Society. Other group tours

should be scheduled through the First Church Property Manager or Office Manager.

A detailed map and directions are readily available at the Wethersfield Historical Society website.

Above: First Church, Wethersfield

Left: A replica of Jonathan Edwards' swivel reading desk in the Jonathan Edwards room in the First Church of Wethersfield. The original is in Stockbridge

❷ Pursuing the glory of God

Jonathan Edwards' Puritan heritage revealed itself in his seventy written resolves to live passionately, and with every breath, for the glory of God. These resolutions set the tone for much of his life and ministry to come

In August of 1722 the young Jonathan Edwards, not yet 19 years old, made the journey to New York City to take up pastoral responsibilities in a small Presbyterian congregation. While he was serving this congregation, it acquired a building on William Street between Wall Street and Liberty Street (then Crown Street) in what is now Lower Manhattan. This small gathering had broken away from a larger congregation over issues related to pastoral authority.

New York would have been very different from any other town the young Edwards had visited. Growing up in the Connecticut River valley he had been exposed to one homogenous culture: that of English Puritanism transplanted into the New World. Growing up in Timothy Edwards' home would have introduced him to African-Americans, since the Edwards family always owned an African slave. There would also have been the presence, sometimes dangerous, of the Native American culture. But essentially Edwards had grown up in a fairly uniform culture.

New York was different. The Dutch had founded it in 1624 as a trading post, and originally it was called New Amsterdam until the British took it over in 1664, when it was renamed New York. By the 1720s the town was a cosmopolitan centre of some seven to ten thousand people, drawn from a variety of backgrounds: obviously Dutch and British, but also French

Above: The port of New York in the eighteenth century

Facing page: The present Meeting House of the First Church of New Haven. During Jonathan Edwards' days at Yale he would have worshipped with the First Church as would James Pierpont, his fellow tutor and son to its former pastor

Left: Forbes Library, Northampton, Mass. houses a small number of Stoddard's and Edwards' manuscripts

Protestants (known as Huguenots who had fled France because of religious persecution), German Lutherans, a significant number of African Americans, and even some Jews—who would have been descendants of the Sephardic Jews who came to New York from Brazil in 1654. Edwards later referred to one Jewish man in particular who impressed him with his outward religious devotion.

Being away from familiar surroundings gave the young Edwards time to reflect on his calling and personal walk with God. It would be during this particular period of Edwards' life that he began to lay detailed plans for his private pursuit of godliness.

The Resolutions

While in New York, Edwards became increasingly conscious of the sin that lay deeply entwined in the depths of the human heart and thus the ease with which deception could occur with regard to personal growth in holiness. As an antidote, Edwards began to record a series of resolutions to review regularly in order to remind himself of those areas of his life that needed his constant care and attention. He eventually recorded seventy in all, to help keep him passionate in his pursuit of God and his glory (see page 122–126) for the full list).

The value of these Resolutions has long been recognized— evidenced by the numerous reprints of them during the past three hundred years. Though young as a Christian when he wrote them, they reveal a mature understanding of genuine piety and the way such godliness should be evident in all of life. In Resolution 26, for example, he 'resolved, to cast away such things as I find do abate my assurance [of salvation].' Resolution 40, written on 7 January 1723, subjected his eating and drinking habits to scrutiny: 'Resolved, to inquire every night, before I go to bed, whether I have acted in the best way I possibly could, with respect to eating and drinking.' The final resolution, Resolution 70, recognizes the importance of being circumspect in all his speech: 'Let there be something of benevolence in all that I speak.'

Some of the Resolutions are more general than these. For example, in the first one Edwards resolved, 'That I will do whatsoever I think to be most to the glory of God and my own good, profit and pleasure, in the whole of my duration; without any consideration of the time, whether now, or never so many myriad of ages hence. Resolved to do whatever I think to be my duty, and most for the good and advantage of mankind in general. Resolved, so to do, whatever difficulties I meet with, how many soever, and how great soever.'

These Resolutions reveal Edwards' clear grasp of a very important truth, one that Edwards' New England Puritan forebears also knew very well: a close walk with God entails resolute commitment, ardency of desire and firm discipline.

The setting for much of this probing of the human heart took place north of the city along the banks of the Hudson River where, Edwards tells us, he 'very frequently used to retire into a solitary place ... for contemplation of divine things

---

New England Puritanism

Puritanism in New England can be traced back to two settlements. The first consisted of those stricter Puritans called Separatists who had given up trying to reform the Church of England. They formed their own congregations independent of the Church of England and regarded that church as a false church. These Puritans crossed the Atlantic in 1620, heading for Virginia. Blown off course they landed eventually at Plymouth in Cape Cod Bay after sixty-six days at sea. This colony was eventually absorbed into the other Puritan colony, namely, Massachusetts, in 1691.

The very first settlers of the Massachusetts Bay colony had landed at Salem in 1628. Unlike the Separatists at Plymouth Plantation, these Puritans and the other founders of the Massachusetts Bay colony were Puritan Congregationalists who had remained within the Church of England, seeking to reform her from within. All of the first ministers in this colony had been ordained within the Church of England.

Among these early ministers in the colony was John Cotton (1584–1652), who had been the parish minister in Boston, Lincolnshire, before his emigration in 1633 to Massachusetts. In the new world he settled at Boston, where, not long after his arrival, he became the minister of the church there. In time he became one of the leading architects of New England Congregationalism, defending its baptism of infants against the Baptists, and its congregational church government against the Presbyterians and their rule by elders. Many New Englanders found his book *The Keyes of the Kingdom of Heaven* (1644) a persuasive presentation of Congregationalism.

and secret converse with God.' At the same time, he would gaze with delight upon the world of nature: river and trees and shrubs—so different a scene than now in that same locale—and see in it the power and might of a sovereign and loving God.

The *Miscellanies*

While the young pastor was drawing up his Resolutions he also began to pen a set of notebooks called the *Miscellanies*. In these various notebooks he carefully recorded his thoughts, questions, and observations on the Bible, philosophy and the world in general. Developed throughout his life, these notebooks were individually lettered at first and later numbered and copiously cross-referenced in an index.

The *Miscellanies* reveal a man whose deep reflection was not simply personal and experiential but profoundly theological. The very first of these entries was recorded during this period of

his life in New York and is an extended theological reflection on holiness. 'Holiness is a most beautiful and lovely thing,' Edwards wrote. 'We drink in strange notions of holiness from

Below: Bolton historical marker; Edwards pastored here briefly in the early 1720s

Bottom: The current building of the Bolton Congregational Church where Edwards pastored

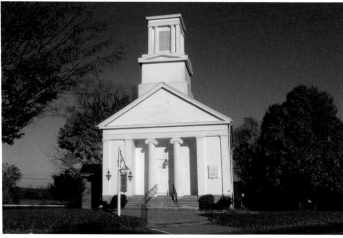

our childhood, as if it were a melancholy, morose, sour and unpleasant thing; but there is nothing in it but what is sweet and ravishingly lovely. 'Tis the highest beauty and amiableness, vastly above all beauties. ... 'Tis almost too high a beauty for any creatures to be adorned with; it makes the soul a little, sweet and delightful image of the blessed Jehovah.' Edwards' evident delight in holiness would give shape to his later life.

The New York pastorate, though brief in time, proved to be an extremely fruitful time in the personal life of the young minister. His later preaching from the Bible and influential works of doctrine were rooted in these times of quiet meditation and solitude, the value of which he knew first on the banks of the Hudson River. Despite the desire of some in the New York church to have Edwards stay on as their pastor, and Edwards' close friendship with many in the congregation, he left New York in the spring of 1723. His father had been influential in having him called to a Congregationalist church in Bolton, only fifteen miles away from East Windsor. So it was with deep reluctance that Edwards left New York—'most bitter' are the words he uses to describe his feelings upon leaving—and arrived home on 1 May.

The short respite in his parents' East Windsor home gave him time to complete a couple of significant projects. In the summer months of July and August he finished his Master's thesis (called a Quaestio in Latin) on one of the great themes of the Reformation: justification by faith alone. True to the Reformed tradition of New England Puritanism, Edwards agued from the Scriptures that 'a sinner is not justified in the sight of God except through the righteousness of Christ obtained by faith.' The formal presentation of this thesis would be at the public commencement at Yale in September, only one year after the defection of Cutler and others to Anglicanism.

Another project that was completed during this time was the now-famous 'Spider' letter, probably written in October 1723. Edwards showed his scientific ability by carefully observing and recording some experiments relative to certain spiders common in East Windsor. He observed how they managed to appear to fly by use of an almost invisible filament and were able to travel from tree to tree in this fashion. The letter was composed for hopeful publication by the Royal Society in London in its Philosophical Transactions. This material reveals that Edwards, though now devoted to the pursuit of pastoral life, was not without other thoughts about his possible future.

It is interesting that his father, who appears to have liked to have his son in close geographical proximity—hence bringing him to the pastorate in Bolton—has a note on one of his sermons from 1722 that indicates the younger Edwards had raised the idea of his going to study in London. The subject may well have come up

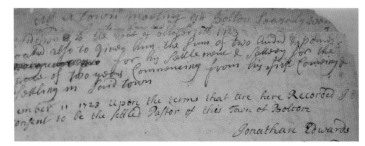

Above: The signature of Edwards from the Town Records at Bolton, CT accepting the call to be the town's congregational minister in 1723

Below: A field in Bolton viewed from the site of the Old Parsonage where Edwards lived

again during this time at home with his parents in the summer of 1723. For students like Edwards, London was the intellectual centre of the English-speaking world. But if the note is anything to go by, his father's reaction was quite negative to this proposal. Timothy wrote three words in the following order that may speak volumes about any idea of his son going across the Atlantic: 'Jonathan. London. Corruption.'

At the close of the summer and after the harvest in East Windsor, Edwards made the short trek to Bolton, Connecticut. There is clear evidence that he really did not take up this new ministry with enthusiasm. It was a duty that his father especially expected him to do and he was resolved by God's grace to do that duty. But like his time in New York, this also was to be a short pastorate. He settled at Bolton in November. His signature on the town records, agreeing to be the community's pastor, appears for 11 November 1723. Bolton, like New York, provided opportunity to continue Edwards' growth in grace, as entries from a Diary he kept from 1722 to 1725 reveal. Now instead of the banks of the Hudson, he had fields to roam in for the times of quiet meditation.

A Yale tutor

In late May 1724 Edwards was offered a tutorship at his old college, Yale. It commenced

Above and left: *The entrance to Jonathan Edwards College at Yale established in 1932. It is here that the Badger portraits of Jonathan and Sarah Edwards are housed*

in June of 1724 and provided mixed experiences for the young Edwards. On the one hand, it gave him access to one of the most well-stocked libraries in Connecticut. Edwards was ever eager to read the latest works being written by various European authors: men like the great physicist Isaac Newton and the philosopher John Locke. But he especially delighted to pore over the theological tomes

of the seventeenth century written by men like Richard Sibbes, John Owen—two great Puritan authors—and Peter van Mastricht, a leading Dutch Calvinist theologian. 'Take Mastricht,' Edwards could say, 'for divinity [that is, theology] in general, doctrine, practice, and controversy … it is much better than … any other book in the world, excepting the Bible, in my opinion.'

Right: *Beinecke Rare Book and Manuscript Library at Yale University. Many of the volumes Edwards studied are now housed here. Additionally there is a copy of the Guttenberg Bible*

Above: The window over the entrance to the present Meeting House of the First Church in New Haven

On the other hand, there was the loss of time for meditation and contemplation. Students were expected to apply themselves to their studies six days a week. The day began at 6 am and proceeded under structured times until supper at 5 pm. Throughout this time-frame Jonathan would be required to hear extended recitations from the students on various subjects. Additionally, the college was still in some managerial disarray as a new Rector had not yet been found to replace Cutler, and so Jonathan and his fellow tutor James Pierpont were largely responsible for all the college duties relative to forty to fifty budding scholars who had all the unruly behaviour and folly that marks out students in any era.

Jonathan's stark realization of these differences is evident from his first record upon arriving in New Haven. Writing in the evening of Saturday 6 June, Edwards noted in his Diary that 'this week has been a very remarkable week with me, with respect to despondencies, fears, perplexities, multitudes of cares, and distraction of mind … I have now abundant reason to be convinced of the troublesomeness and vexation of the world, and that it never will be another kind of world.' The following weeks seem to have brought little relief. At the end of September he noted that the 'hurries of commencement' and the fact that there was still no Rector had 'been the occasion of my sinking so exceedingly, as in the three last weeks.'

The challenge of teaching and managing the lives of some of these students brought out the worst in Edwards as he noted in a Diary entry for 16 February 1724: 'A virtue which I need in a higher degree, to give a beauty and lustre to my behaviour, is gentleness. If I had more of an air of gentleness, I should be much mended.' Dealing with such heart struggles would be of great value in shaping the pastor that Edwards would become. However, these challenges took a toll on Edwards, who was never a robust man. He fell ill in the autumn of 1725 and went back to convalesce at East Windsor. He returned to his duties in mid-summer of 1726, but not for long. That August he was asked to become assistant pastor at his maternal grandfather's church in Northampton, Massachusetts.

Coming to Northampton

Edwards' maternal grandfather was Solomon Stoddard, who occupied the most significant New England pulpit outside Boston. Stoddard, a man of remarkable talent, was pastor in Northampton from 1669 until his death in 1729, and was sometimes described by his theological opponents as a 'congregational Pope'. As Edwards later remarked, the people of Northampton came to consider Stoddard 'almost as a sort of deity'. While Stoddard retained his power of speech up to the end of his long life, his eyesight and hearing began to fail in the mid-1720s. The church thus began to look for an assistant for their venerable pastor, and their thoughts turned to the pastor's grandson.

Above: Stoddard's Northampton home as it now appears

Below: Connecticut River near the old ferry crossing in Northampton, Massachusetts

Edwards resigned his tutorship in September, and the following month he travelled to Northampton for a trial period of preaching in this pivotal pastoral charge. A month or so later, on 21 November, he was voted in as assistant to his grandfather and given 50 acres of land, £300 to build a home (on King Street

as it turned out), and £100 a year as salary. Presumably up until that point he had lived in his grandfather's home that was set on a hill overlooking the town. The following year, on 15 February, Edwards was duly ordained as pastor. His earlier ministries in New York and Bolton had been as an unordained preacher. If he had stayed long enough in either of these two places he would have been formally ordained at some point. Edwards had the benefit of the older man's counsel for just under two years before, on 11 February 1727, the Northampton patriarch died.

His death was 'like the falling of a mighty spreading tree ... A wide breech has been made', said

Above: The graves of Solomon Stoddard, his wife Esther Warham Mather Stoddard (Jonathan Edwards' Grandparents) and the Stoddards' son, Col. John Stoddard, in the Bridge Street Cemetery, Northampton, MA

William Williams, Stoddard's son-in-law and thus Edwards' uncle, who preached the funeral sermon for Stoddard. Who knew how long it would be before that great tree's place was filled again? Little did he, or any of his hearers know, that in their midst was one destined to be a much greater preacher and theologian than the venerable pastor whose life had just come to a close.

TRAVEL INFORMATION

Bolton, CT

222 Bolton Center Road, Bolton, CT 06043, ☎ 860–649–8066.

Bolton, CT was originally a part of Hartford known as Hanover or Hartford Mountains and was incorporated as a separate community in 1720 being named after Bolton, England. The first meeting house construction was begun in 1721 and the first minister to be extended a call was Jonathan Edwards who signed the town record book on 11 November 1723 accepting the call. His pastorate was short lived as Jonathan accepted an appointment as tutor at Yale a few months later. The first truly settled minister was Rev Thomas White in 1725. The current building is situated across from the green in the center of town where the original church structure

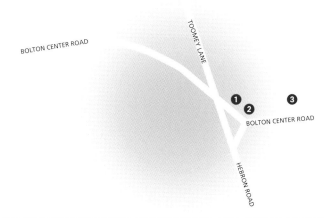

BOLTON, CT

1 TOWN HALL
2 BOLTON CONGREGATIONAL CHURCH

3 SITE OF THE OLD PARSONAGE

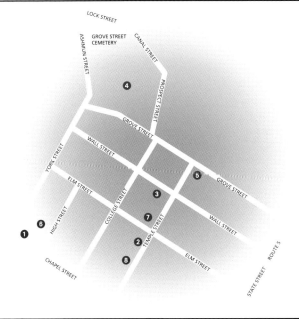

NEW HAVEN, CT

1 YALE UNIVERSITY ART GALLERY
2 NORTH CHURCH NEW HAVEN GREEN
3 BEINECKE RARE BOOK & MANUSCRIPT
  LIBRARY
4 GROVE ST CEMETERY

5 TIMOTHY DWIGHT COLLEGE
6 JONATHAN EDWARDS COLLEGE
7 VISITOR CENTER
8 CENTER CHURCH ON THE GREEN
  CRYPT IN BASEMENT

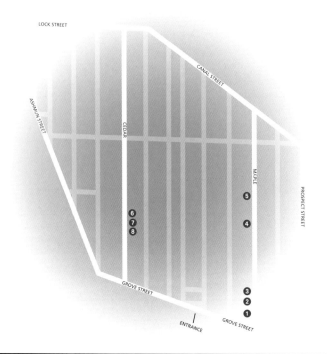

NEW HAVEN CEMETERY

1 EZRA STILES
2 TIMOTHY DWIGHT, SR
3 PIERPONT EDWARDS
4 ROGER SHERMAN

5 THOMAS CLAP
6 NOAH WEBSTER
7 ELI WHITNEY
8 LYMAN BEECHER

stood. Bolton is to this day a small but beautiful New England town.

Bolton Congregational Church UCC

228 Bolton Center Road, Bolton, Connecticut 06043. ☎ 860–649–7077.

The City of New Haven, CT

General travel and tourist information regarding New Haven, CT, and the area, can be found at the following: ww.cityofnewhaven.com/today. There is also a fully staffed info center in downtown New Haven:

1000 Chapel Street, New Haven, CT 06510, ☎ 203–773–9494.

First Church and Crypt

311 Temple Street, New Haven, CT 06511, ☎ 203–787–0121

One fascinating feature of New Haven is the Crypt located under the First Church on the Green. It has stones dating back into the late 1600s. Warning: Watch your head and your step!

Grove Street Cemetery

227 Grove Street, New Haven, CT 06511–6806. ☎ 203–787–1443. See their website.

Established in 1796, this New Haven burying ground is rich with the graves of men such as Pierpont Edwards, youngest son of Jonathan and Sarah, and Timothy Dwight, grandson of Jonathan and Sarah and president of Yale. Additionally there are a number of headstones removed from the old cemetery on the Green that have been cataloged and placed here for display. The website provides information on locations of specific individuals as well as walking tour guides of the cemetery. Directions are also available along with a wealth of additional information.

Yale University

General visitor information regarding Yale University can be obtained at Yale Visitors Center.

149 Elm Street, New Haven CT 06511. ☎ 203–432–2300.

There are no buildings remaining which date to the collegiate days of Jonathan Edwards. The oldest building on campus dates to 1750 and the Jonathan Edwards College is a 20th century addition to the university. Campus tours are available

Above: Ezra Stiles' tomb, a contemporary of Edwards and later President of Yale

through the Visitor Center which include a visit to the Beinecke Rare Book and Manuscript Library of Yale. The original edition of the only portraits of Jonathan and Sarah Edwards are housed in Jonathan Edwards College, one of the colleges of Yale University. Jonathan's desk is also located here. For viewing information contact the Yale Visitor Center.

Above: Timothy Dwight College, Yale University

Beinecke Rare Book and Manuscript Library

Wall Street, New Haven, CT, ☎ 203 432–4047. The Beinecke houses many of Edwards's manuscripts and a rich store of other fascinating books and documents. One of the few remaining Gutenberg Bibles is on display as well. Visitors may view the numerous displays without reservation or special privileges needed. Access to the manuscripts and other non-display material is not available to the general public and must be accessed through the library staff. It is wise to contact them in advance either by phone or via the web as closure dates and hours vary.

A map of New Haven is available at the City website.

❸ 'My Dear Companion'

For many today 'Puritan' implies 'prudish'. But Puritan marriages, like that of Jonathan and Sarah Edwards, were often ruled by passionate love between husband and wife. This was certainly true for Jonathan and Sarah and their love helped shape the lives of their eleven children

Among the families with whom Edwards developed a friendship while he was at Yale was the Pierponts, who were one of the most prominent ministerial families of that part of New England. James Pierpont, Sr., pastor of the Congregational church in New Haven from 1685 till his death in 1714, was a friend of Timothy Edwards as well as being one of the founders of Yale. His congregation long remembered him as being 'eminent in the gift of prayer'. His widow, Mary Hooker Pierpont, was a granddaughter of Thomas Hooker the founding father of Hartford. After her husband's demise, she remained in New Haven with her children. One of her sons, James Pierpont, Jr., was a fellow tutor at Yale along with Jonathan.

Sarah Pierpont

The friendship of Edwards with James Pierpont, which may have included visits to the family home, and the certain contact at worship with the entire Pierpont family, brought a younger sister of James to Edwards' attention. At the onset of his tutorship at Yale in 1723 Sarah Pierpont was just fourteen. When she was older she would be known for her beauty, and Samuel Hopkins, Edwards' first biographer who lived in Jonathan and Sarah Edwards' home for a while, recalled that Sarah was 'comely and beautiful'. Speaking generally of the attractiveness of the opposite sex, Edwards recorded in his *Miscellanies* 189 the following: 'We see how great love the human nature is capable of, not only to God but fellow creatures. How greatly are we inclined to the other sex! Nor doth an exulted

Above: James Pierpont

Facing page: Entrance to Timothy Dwight College at Yale University

and fervent love to God hinder this, but only refines and purifies it.'

This was written in 1725 and one can only speculate if Jonathan was thinking of Sarah at the time. Jonathan's first clearly recorded words about his future wife were inscribed in the front page of a Greek grammar in 1723. Sarah was obviously too young for Edwards to court. Yet he could still pen a record of his admiring love:

'They say there is a young lady in [New Haven] who is beloved of that almighty Being, who made and rules the world, and that there are certain seasons in which this Great Being, in some way or other invisible, comes to her and fills her mind with exceeding sweet delight, and that she hardly cares for any thing, except to meditate on him—that she expects after a while to be received up where he is, to be raised out of the world and caught up into heaven; being assured that he loves her too well to let her remain at a distance from him always. There she is to dwell with him, and to be ravished with his love, favour and delight for ever. Therefore, if you present all the world before her, with the richest of its treasures, she disregards it and cares not for it, and is unmindful of any pain or affliction. She has a strange sweetness in her mind, and sweetness

Above: *Pierpont's name appears above a doorway at Yale*

Below: *The gravestone of Thomas Hooker in Hartford*

of temper, uncommon purity in her affections; is most just and praiseworthy in all her actions; and you could not persuade her to do anything thought wrong or sinful, if you would give her all the world, lest she should offend this great Being. She is of a wonderful sweetness, calmness and universal benevolence of mind; especially after those times in which this great God has manifested himself to her mind. She will sometimes go about, singing sweetly, from place to [place]; and she seems to be always full of joy and pleasure; and no one know for what. She loves to be alone, and to wander in the fields and on the mountains, and seems to have someone invisible always conversing with her.'

Noteworthy in this small text is the appearance again and again of the word 'sweet' or one of its variants. He mentions Sarah's 'wonderful sweetness,' the 'strange sweetness' of her mind, her sweet temper, her 'singing sweetly', and God filling her with 'exceeding sweet delight'. This was one of Edwards' favourite terms when he spoke of God and divine things. It indicates how central he considered the enjoyment of God to be to the Christian life. Clearly it was Sarah's ardent love of God that attracted Jonathan to his future wife.

Yet, it should be noted, her

Below: *Portrait of Sarah Pierpont Edwards when she was 41*

physical beauty was not without its power over him. As he wrote in his Miscellanies 108 around 1724, and surely he must have been thinking of Sarah: 'When we behold a beautiful body, a lovely proportion, a beautiful harmony of features of face, delightful airs of countenance and voice, and sweet motion and gesture, we are charmed with it.' Among the things that Jonathan and his bride-to-be loved to do during this time of courtship was singing together. As he said at this time: 'The best, most beautiful, and most perfect way that we have of expressing a sweet concord of mind to each other, is by music.'

Marriage

Jonathan and Sarah were married on Friday, 28 July 1727. Samuel Miller, a 19th century author, commented that 'Perhaps no event of Mr Edwards' life had a more close connexion with his subsequent comfort and usefulness than this marriage.' While brilliant in the pulpit and a genius with his pen, Jonathan was really not adept at managing the details of the day-to-day running of his New England household. When Sarah went for a visit to Boston in the summer of 1748, for example, Jonathan wrote to tell

A HOUSE FOR THE TOWNE
1655-1661

Left: A drawing of the First Meeting House in Northampton which had been replaced before Edwards' time

Below left: A drawing of the Second Meeting House in Northampton. It was in this church that Sarah would have sat as a new bride, at the age of seventeen, fully prepared to be reviewed by the people of Northampton

her after a while that he and the children had 'been without you almost as long as we know how to be'. In the words of Samuel Hopkins, Sarah was 'a good economist,' who 'took almost the whole care of the temporal affairs of the family, without doors and within.' See Box: 'The home economics of Sarah Edwards' on page 81.

That letter of Jonathan Edwards referred to in the previous paragraph begins with the phrase 'My Dear Companion'. Throughout their married life Jonathan highly valued his

wife's companionship and help. Her early piety that so attracted Jonathan did not leave her. Samuel Hopkins records that later in life she remained 'eminent for her piety and religious conversation.' Ebenezer Parkman, the minister at Westborough, a town between Northampton and Boston, recorded in his diary for 30 May 1742, when Sarah made an overnight stop in Westborough on the way home from visiting Boston, that he had the pleasure of her conversation. It was 'very wonderful,' he wrote, especially 'her sense of divine things'.

Little wonder that George Whitefield, the remarkable English evangelist, wrote in his Diary on Sunday 19 October 1740, when he visited the Edwards' household: 'A sweeter couple I have not yet seen.' In fact their home made Whitefield think seriously about marriage. He went on to record in his Diary:

'Felt great satisfaction in being at the house of Mr Edwards. … Mrs Edwards is adorned with a meek and quiet spirit; she talked solidly of the things of God, and seemed to be such a helpmeet for her husband, that she caused me to renew those prayers, which, for some months, I have put up to God, that he would be pleased to send me a daughter of Abraham to be my wife.'

The influence of the Edwards home was significant—two years later George married Elizabeth James!

'A little church'

Sarah and Jonathan reared eleven children, and all beyond infancy. In a day when infant mortality was extremely high, this is truly amazing. Cotton Mather, the influential New England Puritan who died in 1728 (see picture on page 85), had fifteen children—but only two lived beyond infancy. Jonathan is frequently portrayed as a stern and implacable father, a picture that is belied by all of the primary sources that we have about the Edwards' family life. Samuel

Puritanism and marriage

'The man whose heart is endeared to the woman he loves,' wrote Thomas Hooker, one of the key founders of Puritan New England, 'he dreams of her in the night, hath her in his eye and apprehension when he awakes, museth on her as he sits at table.' Though not at all the sort of remark that the contemporary world associates with the Puritans, it is actually a typical Puritan sentiment, for the Puritans revelled in the joys of marriage. Marriage, in their minds, was held together by the glue of love, and sex was one of the main ways in which that love expressed itself.

Anne Bradstreet, America's first notable poetess who died in 1672, could thus write of the joy of being married to her husband Simon:

"If ever two were one, then surely we.
If ever man were loved by wife, then thee.
If ever wife was happy in a man,
Compare with me, ye women, if you can.
I prize thy love more than whole mines of gold,
Or all the riches that the East doth hold."

It is noteworthy that Edwards had seen first-hand, in his parents' Puritan home, an example of such conjugal love. In a sermon that he preached on 28 June 1730, Timothy Edwards stressed that a man's love for his wife must be 'a singular, peculiar thing,' in which he was never to abuse his authority as head of the home but to act 'in a loving manner with due respect to his wife.'

Above: All that remains of the Edwards' home in Northampton, New England, is this doorstep!

Below: Jonathan Edwards Jr., the 9th child of Jonathan and Sarah. Like his father, he became a leading theologian in his own right. He died while serving as president of Union College, NY

Hopkins clearly states that his children 'reverenced, esteemed, and loved him'.

Jonathan's role as spiritual mentor to his children had begun when each of them was very small. Hopkins observed that Jonathan 'took opportunities to converse with them in his study, singly and particularly about their own soul's concerns; and to give them warning, exhortation, and direction, as he saw occasion.' In addition to this, Edwards began each day with family prayer, in which he would read a chapter of God's word—often, Hopkins recalled, in the winter this reading would be done by candlelight as the family rose before daybreak—and ask his children questions about the text appropriate to their ages. Every Saturday evening, Jonathan instructed his children in the *Westminster Shorter Catechism*: 'Not merely by taking care that they learned it by heart,' Hopkins observed, 'but by leading them into an understanding of the doctrines therein taught, by asking them questions on each answer, and explaining it to them.' Underlying all of this was Edwards' conviction that 'every Christian family ought to be as it were a little church, consecrated to Christ, and wholly influenced and governed by his rules.'

In terms of discipline, corporal punishment appears to have been a rarity in the Edwards household. Jonathan corrected his children, 'with the greatest calmness, and commonly without striking a blow'. And with regard to Sarah's government of her children, Hopkins notes that she 'seldom struck her children,' but would

reprove them 'in few words, without warmth and noise, but with all calmness and gentleness of mind'.

One fascinating sidelight on the Edwards' home is the family's love of chocolate, evidenced by the numerous notes from Jonathan to friends to buy him chocolate from Boston and elsewhere. Chocolate could be bought in an unsweetened 'cake' form and was used normally as a breakfast beverage. On 28 May 1745, for instance, Jonathan 'sent to Boston by Capt John Lyman £3 for Chocolate'. In September of 1750 a prominent Northampton figure, Elisha Pomeroy, was going up to Boston, and Edwards gave him £7 for '7 pounds of chocolate,' which was an expensive item for that day.

At a time when 18th century New England folk wisdom believed that the day of the week on which one was born was the same day as when one was conceived, it is amusing to note that six of the Edwards children were born on a Sunday—a seventh, Eunice, missed it by a half-hour! Between 1728 and 1740 Jonathan and Sarah had seven children,

Above: A Puritan family

Below: Venetian Noblemen in a Café (drinking chocolate), Jan van Grevenbroeck, (1731–1807) Museo Correr, Venice, Italy The Bridgeman Art Library

each born two years apart. This pattern was broken after the birth of Susannah in 1740. Their next child, Eunice, was born in 1743 and their final three in 1745, 1747, and 1750 respectively.

The first daughter, Sarah, was born in 1728, the year following their marriage. Sarah tended to be sickly as a child, so much so, that when she was staying with relatives in Lebanon, Connecticut, in the summer of 1741, Jonathan told her plainly in a letter that she had 'a very weak and infirm body' and as such she might not live long; if she, therefore, lived for the comforts of this world, she was apt to be disappointed, but, he went on, 'if your soul prospers you will be an happy blessed person, whatever becomes of your body. I wish you much of the presence of Christ and communion with him, and that you might live so as to give him honour in the place where you are by an amiable behaviour towards all.'

As it happened, Sarah would live to the age of seventy-seven! But while her father misjudged Sarah's physical hardiness, his advice about and prayer for her spiritual health well reveal his understanding of his calling as Sarah's father.

The next child was Jerusha, born in 1730. She was the first of the Edwards' children to die, and the circumstances of her death will be discussed in more detail in Chapter 6. Esther was their third child, born in 1732. At the age of twenty she married Aaron Burr, Sr., the second president of the College of New Jersey (later Princeton University), whom Ezra Stiles, a later President of Yale College, called 'an excellent divine and preacher…an eminent

Above: Esther Edwards Burr

Left: Jerusha Edwards' grave in the Bridge Street Cemetery Northampton, alongside that of David Brainerd

Christian and every way the worthy man.' Like her father, Esther had a remarkable piety and infectious love for Christ. Her devotion is well revealed by a Diary that actually forms a series of letters to a close friend by the name of Sarah Prince, the daughter of Thomas Prince, a Boston pastor and friend of her father.

A fourth daughter, Mary, born in 1734, married a judge by the name of Timothy Dwight and lived to be an evangelical 'matriarch'. One letter to her from her father survives. Edwards begins the letter by expressing his concern for Mary's physical well-being, since she was a considerable distance away in Portsmouth, New Hampshire. Yes, he stressed—and now he includes his wife Sarah as a co-writer of the letter:

> 'Though you are at so great a distance from us, yet God is everywhere. …We have not the comfort of seeing you, but he sees you. …And if you may but be sensibly nigh to him, and have his gracious presence, 'tis no matter though you are far distant from us. I had rather you should remain hundreds of miles distant from us and have God nigh to you by his Spirit, than to have you always with us, and live at a distance from God.'

Above: The grave of Aaron Burr Sr. in the Presidents' lot, Princeton Cemetery, Princeton, New Jersey. He was the husband of Esther and second President of the New College at New Jersey, now Princeton University. The column marks the grave of Aaron Burr Jr.

Below: Aaron Burr Jr., son to Esther and Aaron Burr and grandson to Jonathan and Sarah Edwards. Lawyer, statesman and Vice President of the United States under Thomas Jefferson and probably most well known for killing Alexander Hamilton in a duel. He is buried at his father's feet in the Presidents' lot of the Princeton Cemetery

46

Esther Edwards Burr and her diary

Reading Esther's diary reveals that one of the things she prized was spiritual friendship with women like Sarah Prince. Writing on 20 April 1755, for instance, she told Sarah, 'I … highly value … friends that one might unbosom their whole soul to. … I esteem religious conversation one of the best helps to keep up religion in the soul.'

For Esther, true friends were those with whom one could be transparent and open. And in the course of conversation about spiritual things with such friends the believer could find strength and encouragement for living the Christian life. In referring to this type of conversation as 'one of the best helps to keep up religion in the soul,' Esther obviously views it as one of the ways that God the Holy Spirit keeps Christians in fellowship with the Saviour.

There is little doubt that Jonathan and Sarah delighted in having their children around them—Edwards mentions here 'the comfort' of seeing their daughter. But parental love must be kept in its place. Far more important was that God was close to Mary by his Spirit. If that were so—if Mary, in other words, were indwelt by the Spirit of God because she had been converted—then Jonathan and Sarah would be content to have Mary live 'hundreds of miles' away.

Below and inset: The Dwight family plot in Bridge Street Cemetery, Northampton. The two cenotaphs detail the Edwards family and the Dwight family beginning with Mary Edwards Dwight and husband Timothy

Right: The graves of Timothy and Rhoda Edwards in the Stockbridge Massachusetts Cemetery

A fifth daughter, Lucy, was born in 1736. The first son born to Jonathan and Sarah was Timothy, who lived until 1813. Then came another daughter, Susanna. Three years later, yet another daughter, Eunice was born. The second son, Jonathan, Jr., became a significant theologian in his own right and a leader in New England. The final daughter was Elizabeth and the final son Pierpont.

Unhappily, their youngest son, called 'Pinty' by his brothers and sisters, was the one child who did not turn out well, 'an agnostic in a family famous for its fervent Calvinism', as Edwards scholar Kenneth Minkema has recently put it. This would have deeply upset his parents but would not have utterly devastated them. For them family life was not an end in itself but had its ultimate meaning in the enjoyment of God. As Jonathan declared in a sermon, *The Christian Pilgrim*:

'The enjoyment of God is the only happiness with which our souls can be satisfied. To go to heaven, fully to enjoy God, is infinitely better than the most pleasant accommodations here. Fathers and mothers, husbands, wives, or children, or the company of earthly friends, are but shadows; but God is the substance. These are but scattered beams, but God is the sun. These are but streams, but God is the fountain. These are but drops; but God is the ocean.'

Left: The grave of Timothy Dwight in Grove Street Cemetery, New Haven, CT. The inscription is bronzed and in Latin

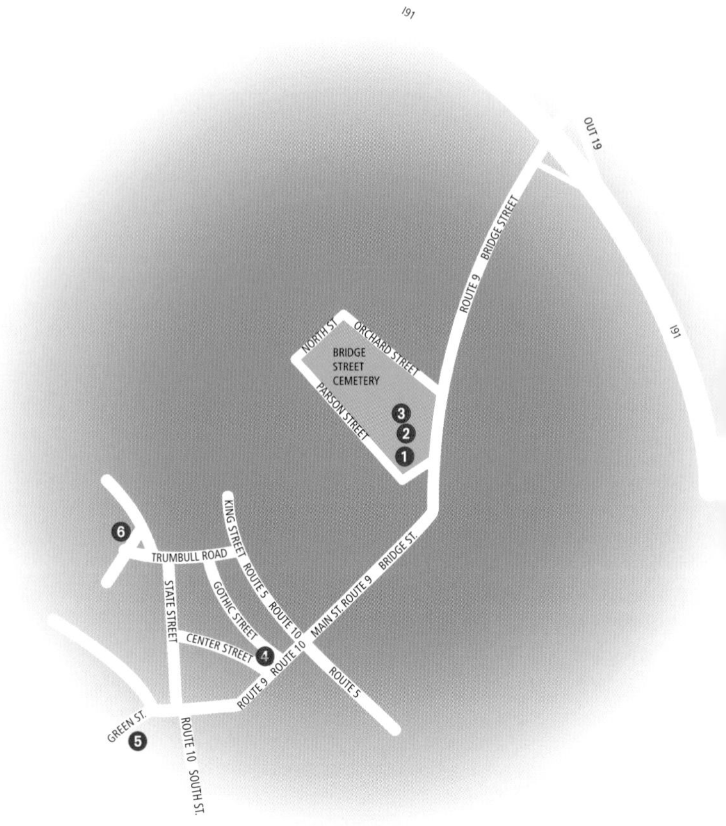

NORTHAMPTON MA

1 EDWARDS' MONUMENT
2 DAVID BRAINARD'S GRAVE
   JERUSHA EDWARDS' GRAVE
3 SOLOMAN STODDARD'S GRAVE

4 FIRST CHURCH
5 FORBES LIBRARY
6 STODDARD'S HOME

TRAVEL INFORMATION

Northhampton, MA

Historic Northampton Museum and Education Center

46 Bridge Street, Northampton, MA 01060, ☎ 413–584–6011.

A wealth of local history and information is available through the museums and shop. The Parsons' House dates from the time of Jonathan Edwards and was owned by one of the members of the family into which Jonathan's daughter Sarah married (Sarah married Elihu Parsons just before Edwards' dismissal from the church in Northampton). Their website and museum include information on Bridge Street Cemetery as well. Contact should be made directly with the museum to assure dates and times of availability.

Forbes Library

20 West St, Northampton, MA 01060. ☎ 413–587–1011.

The Forbes Library is a treasure house of Northampton and Hampshire County history. The building itself is on the Register of Historic Places. While most of Edwards' manuscripts are not housed here, there are still some small documents (i.e. receipts etc.) maintained at Forbes' Hampshire Room for Local History and Special Collections. They have the record books of the Hampshire Association and some Solomon Stoddard manuscripts as well as a number of other historical documents and manuscripts of interest, including Seth Pomeroy's journal of the military engagements at Louisbourg and Crown Point. Pomeroy was a member of the church during Edwards' pastorate in Northampton. It further houses the Calvin Coolidge Presidential Library and Museum. Forbes Library is a public library and it is generally open to the public but availability of material and the particular hours of operation should be obtained directly from the library either via their website or by telephone.

First Churches, UCC & ABC

129 Main Street, Northampton, MA 01060–3145. ☎ 413–584–9392.

The First Churches of Northampton now occupy the fifth meeting house of this historic church founded in 1661. Jonathan Edwards was the third pastor and preached in the Second and Third Meeting Houses. The half-moon entry step to the present structure was the stone step used during Edwards' day (see page 58). Additionally the Church has drawings of the five meeting houses and the sanctuary houses a bronze relief of Jonathan Edwards as well as a chair with his name carved in it. It is important not to confuse this church with the church bearing Edwards' name. The Edwards Church, as it is named, is located a few blocks up Main Street from the First Churches and dates from 1833, well after Edwards' death. For further information and to schedule a tour of the interior of the First Church it will be necessary to contact them directly.

Bridge Street Cemetery

Bridge Street Cemetery contains the graves of Solomon Stoddard, David Brainerd and Jerusha Edwards. There is also Edwards' family plot where Jonathan's daughter Mary is buried and an obelisk listing the family members on the various sides. Jonathan and Sarah are not buried here but are interred in the cemetery in Princeton, New Jersey.

Right: The current building of the First Church, Northampton

4 A surprising work of God

Edwards is rightly known as 'the theologian of revival'.
His theology of revival came from both a solid grasp of
Scripture principles and a deep acquaintance with the
power of the Spirit of God to renew the church and save
those outside of Christ

When Edwards came to the town of Northampton it was on the edge of British civilization: 'Our western frontiers', as Boston newspapers described the land in which it was situated. The town had been founded in 1654 when John Pynchon, a fur trader from Connecticut, had acquired title to the area called Nonotuck (meaning either 'the place in the middle of the river' or 'far away land') from the local native Americans. The area was renamed Northampton as settlers came north from Hartford, Connecticut along the Connecticut River, to develop the new township. The following year they built a meeting house out of 'sawn timber' with a thatched roof that measured 26 feet long and 18 feet wide. They located it at the intersection of the town's two main streets.

This meeting house had been replaced in 1662 by the building that Edwards knew when he first came to Northampton. It was a perfectly square structure with a high turreted roof, measuring 42 feet by 42 feet with two galleries, one of which had been added in 1670 and the other in 1680. It would have been completely without ornamentation and, unlike later meeting houses in Northampton, had no steeple.

Encircling the building were the homes of the town's two hundred or so families. Some of these houses would have been built out of split logs, others were covered with clapboard. None would have been painted. Beyond the homes and protective fortifications, were fields for

THIRD MEETING HOUSE—ERECTED 1737.

Top: Drawing of the third meeting house of Northampton. The drawing hangs on the wall of the First Church in Northampton

Facing page: The interior of First Church, Wethersfield, CT

Above: A copy of the well-known painting of Northampton in Edwards' day which includes the third meeting house in the background

pasture and then the forest that blocked out the horizon. The roads leading out of town became mere tracks once they entered the forest. In the words of Edwards' biographer, Ola Winslow, 'Only the [Connecticut] river led out.'

'Addicted to night-walking'

One of the great areas of concern for Jonathan and Sarah as their children grew up in Northampton were some of the practices among New England youth. When he came to Northampton in 1727, he observed that 'licentiousness for some years [had] prevailed among the youth of the town.' According to Edwards, many of the young people were 'addicted to night-walking, and frequenting the tavern, and lewd practices.' Often they would engage in all-night parties, which they called 'frolics', and had little or no regard for their parents' advice. In fact, Edwards observed, 'Family government did too much fail in the town'.

Edwards would later publicly challenge this practice of 'frolicking' in a sermon on Genesis 39:12 ('And he left his garment in her hand, and fled, and got him out'), which he entitled 'Temptation and Deliverance; or, Joseph's Great Temptation and Gracious Deliverance'. Frolicking, he pointed out, was the cause of 'the most frequent breakings out of gross sins; fornication in particular', and that those who were the most addicted to it were the furthest from any serious profession of Christianity.

Although the Northampton church had enjoyed a number of small spiritual revivals throughout Solomon Stoddard's long pastorate—during his final years of ministry and during the early 1730s—Edwards judged that it was 'a time of extraordinary dullness in religion'. He soon realized that much of the problem lay with the parents of the wayward teenagers. In a sermon that Edwards preached early in 1734, 'Heeding the Word, and Losing It', he clearly laid the responsibility for such behaviour by the young at the door of their parents. He argued, 'When all is said of the degeneracy of young people, it is certainly true that whenever there is a general degeneracy among young people, it is owing very much to parents.'

Many of the parents had given up any attempt at family worship.

Part of the cause of all this, as the new pastor noted, was that the adults in the town were split into two factions. There were those who were wealthy and who had land and influence, and there were those who were not so well off, and who sought to diminish the power and influence of their wealthier neighbours. As a consequence of this, the hearts and thoughts of these adults were taken up, not with God and his eternal kingdom, but with the pursuit of material wealth. They appeared to be orthodox and went to the meeting house week by week, but in reality their orthodoxy was dry and lifeless. Was it any surprise that their children saw their parents' hypocrisy, and responded by outwardly defying their parents' merely external morality?

Signs of a change for the better began to appear in the early 1730s, not long after Edwards had been appointed pastor. There was

Above: *The Parsons' home in present day Northampton. Edwards would have visited the Parsons family in this house*

Right: *The Parsons were a large and prominent family in Northampton as the Parsons' monument evidences. Edwards' daughter, Sarah, married Elihu Parsons*

definitely a growing sensitivity to what God regarded as sin, and a corresponding willingness to listen to spiritual counsel from the pulpit. In November 1734 Edwards preached two sermons on being justified by faith alone, in which he maintained that a living relationship with God is based on trust in the atoning death of Christ for sinners and the gift of his righteousness to all who believe. It cannot be based on human virtue since before a person is a genuine Christian, that person is seen by God as 'an ungodly creature'. Such preaching deeply humbled those who were trusting in their religious inheritance or their own morality for salvation.

There were some in the neighbouring town of Hatfield, Edwards' own cousins the Williams for example, who were critical of these sermons. Israel Williams, an influential merchant in the community, appears to have deeply disliked the sentiments Edwards expressed and from this point onwards his opposition became 'direct and violent'. However, in the providence of God, these sermons were the very thing that people in Northampton needed to hear. As Edwards expressed it later, they turned out to be 'a word spoken in season' and 'attended with a very remarkable blessing of heaven to the souls of the people' in Northampton.

This 'remarkable blessing' was also preceded by the conversion of a woman known for her immoral ways in the town. Edwards referred to her as 'one of the greatest company-keepers in the whole town'—an evident euphemism! Even Edwards himself was surprised when she came to him and related how she had become a Christian. Her conversion caused many to ask her what had happened to her, and the pastor could claim that God made her experience 'the greatest occasion of awakening to others'.

Revival!

In the six months following Edwards' sermons on justification—from December 1734 to the beginning of June 1735—many in Northampton underwent a profound change of heart and a radical shift in their values and ambitions. Edwards claimed, 'Although people did not ordinarily neglect their worldly business, yet religion was with all sorts the great concern, and the world was a thing only by the bye.' Small groups flourished in the town as men and women began to meet informally for prayer and spiritual counsel. Historically such groups had been a central part of Puritan spirituality, and in encouraging these groups to meet, Edwards was tapping into a rich vein of his Puritan heritage.

The alteration in the town and church meetings was dramatic. The town, Edwards observed, 'seemed to be full of the presence of God: it never was so full of love, nor of joy, and yet so full of distress, as it was then.' Few homes remained untouched by the revival as parents and children were converted and husbands and wives gave up following their own ambitions and gave their hearts to God. For a Puritan like Edwards, who believed that Sunday was the divinely appointed day for worship, these six months were nothing less than a taste of heaven: 'God's day was a delight,' he later wrote, and the times of worship 'beautiful.' No one could help noticing that in worship during these months the 'congregation was alive in God's service, every one earnestly intent on the public worship, every hearer eager to drink in the words of the minister as they came from his mouth.'

Edwards initially reckoned that a quarter of the town; some three hundred people were converted in these six months. During March and April 1735, which was probably the height of the revival, there were roughly thirty people a week professing conversion. The converts included around thirty children under the age of fourteen—one of whom, Phoebe Bartlett, was only four, and a goodly number of elderly people, including one woman who was over seventy. Edwards would later believe that there were not as many converts as he had first thought, because some of these conversions were spurious and

had been nothing more than mere emotion. However, overall he never doubted that what had happened during these six months was a tremendous, God-wrought awakening in the town.

Among the youth of the town, Thursday night meetings for pursuing the things of God had become common, with a number of the young men of Northampton urging other young people to attend these meetings for prayer and spiritual encouragement. There was a

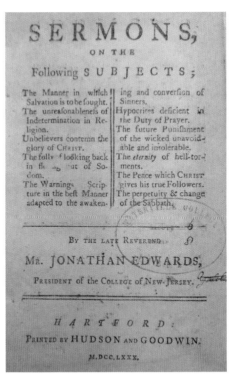

Above: Edwards' sermons were still being published long after his death and are widely read even today. This title page is dated 1780

profound transformation of many of these young people.

Unlike previous revivals in Northampton under the preaching of Solomon Stoddard, which had remained very much local in-town affairs, this revival spread swiftly to towns up and down the Connecticut River Valley. It even reached as far as New Haven and Connecticut towns on the Atlantic coast.

Jonathan Edwards' first publications

Jonathan Edwards' first published work had been a lecture that he gave in Boston in 1731, *God Glorified in the Work of Redemption*, which was a robust defence of God's total sovereignty over all things, especially when it came to salvation. It was a harbinger of other work to come, both in terms of content and kind. Like the tomes and folios of many of his Puritan forebears, most of Edwards' writings were originally sermons. His next major work, though, was not. It was historical narrative, an account of the 1734–1735 revival. Entitled *A Faithful Narrative of a Surprising Work of God*, it was first published in London in 1737, largely through the agency of Benjamin Colman, the cultured pastor of Boston's Brattle Street Congregationalist Church, and the London minister Isaac Watts, the father of English hymnody.

Above: *Title page to* A Faithful Narrative

Left: *Portrait of Benjamin Colman*

This publication made Edwards known to a transatlantic readership and provided inspiration for those labouring and longing for revival elsewhere and especially in Britain. Among those who read it at that time was the Methodist preacher John Wesley who noted in his *Journal*

Above: *Isaac Watts' tomb in Bunhill Fields London, England*

that he read the book while walking to Oxford in October 1738. 'Surely,' he wrote, quoting from Psalm 118, 'this is the Lord's doing, and it is marvellous in our eyes.' Also deeply impressed by the Edwards' account of the revival was Howel Harris, the Welsh Calvinistic Methodist evangelist, who obtained a copy of the book in February 1738. After reading it, he was led to pray, 'O go on with Thy work there [i.e. in New England] and here.' Harris' prayer would receive an answer in 1740–1742, when New England experienced a much more extensive revival. *A Faithful Narrative* also reached into the heart of rural England. In the church records of Waltham Abbey Baptist Church, Essex, there is a reference to the purchase on 12 November 1737 of '2 Hists. of remark Convers. in N. England.' The cost was 2 shillings.

The meeting house controversy

The revival in Northampton came to a sudden end on 1 June 1736, when one of the leading citizens, Joseph Hawley II, an uncle of Edwards by marriage, committed suicide by slitting his throat. It appears that he had become mentally unbalanced during the revival and had fallen prey to depression that ran in his family. Wrongly convinced that there was no spiritual hope for him, he had decided to take his life. His son, Joseph Hawley III, later became one of Edwards' leading opponents in the town and perhaps he blamed the preaching of his cousin for his father's death.

While there had been a great change in the hearts and minds of many of the citizens of Northampton, subsequent events revealed that differences among them could still produce strife, even bitterness. In the years that immediately followed the revival, the most strife was caused by the building of a new meeting house. Owing to decay in the condition

Left: The Half-Moon step to the current meeting house in Northampton is from the third meeting house of Edwards' day

of their meeting house, the townspeople had decided to build a new one in 1737. At the heart of the dispute was the hierarchical nature of New England society, a carry-over from England. Should seating be mainly determined by age—the older being given preference because of infirmity—or wealth and social status? Edwards was deeply distressed when social status was made the major criterion in seat assignment, with the wealthier families being given the better seats. Along with the disputes about the seating arrangement, came the decision in March 1738 to build a separate town hall so that the new meeting house would be seen as a holy space. This was a clear break with the Puritan view of the building used for worship. (See Box on New England meeting houses).

Heaven Is a World of Love

The revival in Northampton gave Edwards a deepened vision of God's redemptive work in Christ as the key to history, which bore fruit in a series of sermons preached in 1739 and which were later published posthumously as *The History of the Work of Redemption* (1774). The previous year, between April and October, he had also given a series on divine love from 1 Corinthians 13. This series also appeared

Right: The First Church of Wethersfield, CT

New England meeting houses

In most New England towns and villages the central architectural feature was the meeting house, which served not only as a place of worship but also as a town hall. This reflected Puritan convictions that, as American historian George Marsden has put it in his masterful biography of Edwards: 'All of reality was potentially sacred or secular, depending on how it was used.' As Marsden further notes, the separation of the meeting house and the town hall can be seen as a harbinger of the modern view that sacred and secular are to exist in separate spheres.

The design of many of the early New England Puritan places of worship owed more to English market halls and guildhalls than to English parish churches. These buildings were not viewed as being or containing sacred space—thus their use as town halls during the week. To reinforce this conviction, New England Puritanism removed any hint of religious ornamentation from the interior of their meeting houses. Moreover, in

Above and below: *The Old Ship Church Meeting House in Hingham, Massachusetts was erected in 1681 and is typical of 17th century New England meeting houses. It is the oldest church structure in the United States*

speaking of these places of worship, the Puritans never referred to them as churches, but called them 'meeting houses' or simply, 'the meeting'.

The focus on Scripture in Puritanism made the preaching of the Bible central to worship. Architectural prominence within the meeting house was thus given to the pulpit so that it was well within the sight and sound of the entire congregation.

The ideal here was expressed by the English architect Christopher Wren (1632–1723). In a letter that he wrote in 1708, he stressed that it is necessary for everyone practicing the 'Reformed religion ... to hear the service, and both to hear distinctly, and see the preacher.'

Above: The Rocky Hill Meeting House in Amesbury, Massachusetts was constructed in 1785 and is typical of the style of 18th century meeting houses built by New England Puritans. The practice of painting them did not begin until the latter half of that century

Below: The pulpit from the First Church of Wethersfield, Connecticut built in the 1790s shows the centrality and prominence of the preaching of the word of God

posthumously, being published in 1852 as *Charity and Its Fruits*.

The final sermon in this series on 1 Corinthians, *Heaven Is a World of Love*, is one that has been greatly overlooked in evaluations of Edwards. Against the backdrop of the disharmony in Northampton, Edwards argued that heaven was a place of true love and eternal harmony, a result of God, 'the fountain of love, this eternal three in one', flowing out, as it were, 'in streams and rivers of love and delight, enough for all to drink at, and to swim in.'

Edwards has been largely remembered in the history of American literature for his sermon on hellfire, *Sinners in the Hands of an Angry God* (1741), which we will consider in the next chapter. But using this sermon as the main window through which to view Edwards inevitably leads to distortion. As historian David Levin pointed out in 1960: 'Hellfire is not his [Edwards'] characteristic mode of preaching.' The real Edwards is also the man who preached *Heaven Is a World of Love*, an undeniably brilliant portrayal of heaven as a 'land of light and love' and an exhortation to his hearers to live lives of love rooted in God's grace, for as Edwards concluded in his sermon: 'If ever you arrive at heaven, faith and love must be the wings which must carry you there.'

TRAVEL INFORMATION

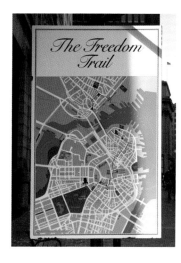

Boston, Massachusetts

Boston has a plethora of historic sites, many of them part of the Freedom Trail, a walking tour of Boston with special reference to Colonial Boston and the American Revolution. Information and an online map can be obtained from the National Park Service. They maintain a facility adjacent to the Old Statehouse. The staff are helpful and knowledgeable. Guided walking tours of the Freedom Trail and other historic information can also be found at The Freedom Trail Foundation (www.thefreedomtrail.org). The walking tours include Copps Hill Burying Ground (Increase and Cotton Mather are buried here along with Phyllis Wheatley in an unmarked grave), Old South Meeting House, the Old North Church (Timothy Cutler, former Yale rector, is buried here. When Jonathan Edwards was a student Cutler 'defected' to Anglicanism and after receiving ordination in England returned to become the first pastor of this historic church). The Walking Tour will also take you to Boston Common, where George Whitefield preached to a thronging crowd during the Great Awakening.

Old South Meeting house

310 Washington St, Boston, MA, 02108.
☎ 617–482–6439.

Jonathan Edwards was friends with Thomas Prince, pastor of Old South Meeting House. Phillis Wheatley, the first African-American poetess and first African-American woman to publish her own writing, was a member here. This historic building is included in the Freedom Trail but also has its own museum and tours. It is a wonderfully restored example of an eighteenth century meeting house. There is a charge to tour the facility and museum. For general travel around Boston, subway and other transit information see www.mbta.com.

Above: *The Old South Meeting House*

❺ Real revival and true fanaticism

Spiritual revivals of the Christian faith transform churches, communities and even nations. Unbelievers are converted and God's people refreshed and renewed in their love and zeal for God and his kingdom—but they are never simple, tidy affairs as Jonathan Edwards understood so well in Northampton, New England

The spiritual lethargy that had afflicted the Northampton community at the time of Edwards' installation as the pastor there was not unique to that community. In the rest of New England the spread of material wealth and the increased availability of luxury items had led to a growing materialism. Far too many of the young were marked by frivolity and indifference to spiritual matters. And there was a noticeable decay of respect for church ministers, as well as a profound sense of spiritual powerlessness. William Cooper, the assistant of Benjamin Colman at Brattle Street Church, Boston, would write in his 'Preface' to Edwards' book *The Distinguishing Marks of a Work of the Spirit of God* (1741): 'What a dead and barren time has it now been, for a great while, with all the churches of the Reformation. The golden showers have been restrained; the influences of the Spirit suspended; and the consequence has been that the Gospel has not had any

eminent success; conversions have been rare and dubious; few sons and daughters have been born to God; and the hearts of Christians not so quickened, warmed and refreshed under the ordinances, as they have been.'

Across the Atlantic, in the heart of the British Empire in England and Wales, things were worse. The state church was led by bishops who were essentially politicians, not men of the Spirit. English historian J. H. Plumb states, 'There is a worldliness

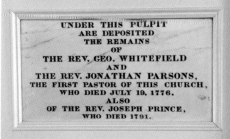

Above: *The plaque on the pulpit at Old South Meeting House*

Facing page: *George Whitefield's body is entombed under this pulpit in the Old South Meeting House in Newburyport, MA*

about eighteenth-century [bishops] which no amount of apologetics can conceal.' Given such leaders, it is not surprising to find that far too many of the clergy under them were addicted to focusing on anything but pastoral ministry and spiritual nurture. Philosophy, botany, agriculture, politics, fox-hunting, drinking and even gambling— all can be found claiming the time and energy of 18th century Anglican clergymen, anything but the gospel of Jesus Christ.

There were a number of Anglican ministers who took seriously their role as spiritual guides, but most of their public preaching and teaching was largely ineffective moralizing. It lacked what historian Horton Davies has called 'any element of holy excitement, of passionate pleading, of heroic challenge, of winged imagination'. Any tinge of spiritual passion was labelled 'enthusiasm' or 'fanaticism'. An inscription on an English tombstone from the period well captures the spiritual ideal of many in the era: 'pious without enthusiasm'. No fire in the pulpit meant neither warmth nor light in the pew; and neither warmth nor light in the pew meant cold-heartedness and spiritual darkness in society at large.

In New England, it was hoped that godly magistrates would arise to check the growth of spiritual indifference and moral decay, but such men failed to materialize. By the 1720s many English-speaking Christians on both sides of the Atlantic were increasingly convinced that the solution to their social and moral problems was revival. The beginning of the answer to the prayers and hopes of these believers came in the revival in Northampton, New England. It is little wonder that Edwards' book on the revival there became such a well-read item on both sides of the Atlantic.

Transatlantic revival and the ministry of George Whitefield

By a neat coincidence, in the same year as the Northampton revival, 1735, the two men who were to be the leaders of the revival in Wales—Howel Harris and Daniel Rowland—were

Above: *Portrait of George Whitefield*

Above: *The day before reaching Northampton, Whitefield preached in what is now West Brookfield, atop this rock on Foster Hill Road*

Right: *The rock is engraved with Whitfield's name and the year 1742*

both converted and began to preach on the new birth and regeneration with amazing power. By 1750 their preaching, and that of others like Howel Davies and William Williams of Pantycelyn—the author of the popular hymn 'Guide me, O thou great Jehovah'—had brought about the creation of 433 religious societies. Known to history as the Calvinistic Methodists, these societies would play a vital role in setting the tone and character of the Welsh people for the next two centuries.

1735 also saw the conversion of George Whitefield, who, more than any other figure, was the one evangelist regarded by the 18th century as the leader in what is known as the Evangelical Revival or Great Awakening in both Great Britain and America. Over the 35 years between his ordination as an Anglican deacon in 1735 and his death in 1770 in Newburyport, Massachusetts, it is calculated that Whitefield preached around 18,000 sermons. Many of these sermons were delivered to congregations in the open air that numbered 10,000 or more.

In addition to his preaching throughout the length and breadth of England, Whitefield regularly itinerated throughout Wales and journeyed fourteen times to Scotland. A number of the ministers who became Whitefield's strongest Scottish supporters—men like William McCulloch of Cambuslang near Glasgow, James Robe of

Kilsyth, and John Erskine of Kirkintilloch, later of Greyfriars Kirk in Edinburgh—would also become devoted correspondents of Edwards. Whitefield was also in America five times during Edwards' lifetime and he preached in virtually every major town on the Atlantic seaboard.

American historian Harry Stout, commenting on Whitefield's impact on America, notes that it was so pervasive 'that he can justly be styled America's first cultural hero. Before Whitefield, there was no unifying inter-colonial person or event. Indeed, before Whitefield, it is doubtful any name other than royalty was known equally from Boston to Charleston. But by 1750 virtually every American loved and admired Whitefield and saw him as their champion.'

In New England between the years 1740 and 1742, which were the height of the revival in that area of America, Whitefield's ministry and those of a number of other preachers, including Edwards, led to a vast number of conversions. How many is not easy to determine since none of the leading figures in the revival sought to measure the revival's impact in numerical terms. One estimate is between 30,000 and 40,000 conversions, which would mean up to a seventh of the population. These numbers are conjecture, but what is clear is that a major transformation of much of New England took place during these years.

In the middle of the winter of 1740, Jonathan Edwards sat down at his desk to write a letter of invitation to George Whitefield to come and preach for his congregation in Northampton that summer. Whitefield had been in America three and a half months at this point on what was his second trip to America. He arrived in New England, not in the summer as Edwards had hoped, but in mid-September. He quickly threw himself into a breathtaking round of itinerant preaching.

Below: Boston common today

In Boston and its neighbourhood, where he preached for twenty-six days, the response to his ministry was overwhelming. Whitefield's farewell sermon on the town common on 12 October drew more than 20,000 listeners, the largest crowd ever assembled in America to that point in history.

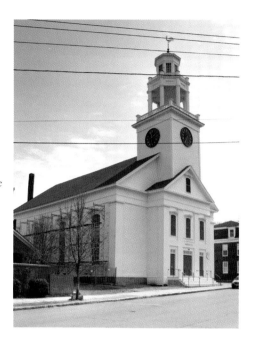

Whitefield spent six days with Edwards, from Friday, 17 October to the following Wednesday, 22 October. As he preached from the Northampton pulpit on the Sunday morning, Whitefield noted in his Diary that 'Edwards wept during the whole time of exercise' and that the congregation were 'equally affected'. In all, Whitefield spoke on five occasions in the town and, Edwards later wrote in 1743, 'The congregation was extraordinarily melted by every sermon', with 'almost the whole assembly being in tears' during the preaching. Whitefield's affective preaching had rekindled the fires of revival in the Massachusetts town.

Top: Meeting House of the First Presbyterian Society in Newburyport, now The Old South Church, erected in 1756 as a direct result of Whitefield's preaching

Above: The monument marking the place of Whitefield's last sermon in Exeter, New Hampshire

Controversy and James Davenport

The Great Awakening, however, was not without its critics, many of whom had embraced the rationalistic worldview of the 18th century Enlightenment and

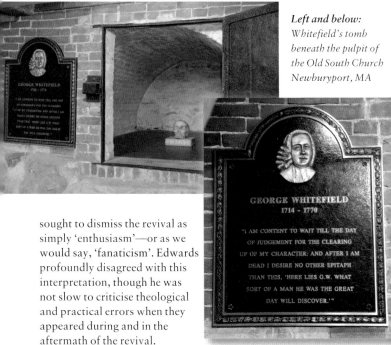

Left and below:
Whitefield's tomb
beneath the pulpit of
the Old South Church
Newburyport, MA

GEORGE WHITEFIELD
1714 - 1770

"I AM CONTENT TO WAIT TILL THE DAY
OF JUDGEMENT FOR THE CLEARING
UP OF MY CHARACTER: AND AFTER I AM
DEAD I DESIRE NO OTHER EPITAPH
THAN THIS, 'HERE LIES G.W. WHAT
SORT OF A MAN HE WAS THE GREAT
DAY WILL DISCOVER.'"

sought to dismiss the revival as simply 'enthusiasm'—or as we would say, 'fanaticism'. Edwards profoundly disagreed with this interpretation, though he was not slow to criticise theological and practical errors when they appeared during and in the aftermath of the revival.

The preaching and example of James Davenport typified these dangerous errors. He was a minister from Southold, Long Island, and came from a distinguished Puritan line. Davenport became acquainted with Whitefield in 1740 in New York and sought to have an itinerant ministry like that of the Englishman. In the course of 1741, however, he began to show signs of extreme fanaticism. He came to believe that he had the gift of knowing who were truly regenerate, and he was not slow

Left: It was in this house, the old parsonage, just down the block from the Old South Church, Newburyport, MA, that Whitefield died from an asthma attack, 30 September 1770

to criticize publicly and by name ministers whom he felt were unconverted. In the summer of 1742 Davenport was in the Boston region, where he spent two months accusing the majority of the Boston ministers of 'leading their people blindfold to hell' and urging their congregations, 'pull them down; turn them out, and put others in their places'. Wherever Davenport went, divided congregations were left in his wake.

Above: Portrait of Charles Chauncy

Davenport's behaviour gave the anti-revival forces, known as the 'Old Lights', a highly visible target for their attacks. To them, Davenport typified all that was wrong with the revival: its revolutionary tendencies and the way that it threatened to destroy church harmony. Captaining the Old Lights was Charles Chauncy, junior pastor of Boston's prestigious First Church. After Edwards' death and long after the Great Awakening, Chauncy would publicly adopt Unitarianism—which denies the Christian doctrine of the Trinity, and Universalism—which argues that no one will go to hell. It would be Edwards' grandson, Timothy Dwight, who would challenge Chauncy's Universalism through the medium of satirical verse. However, at this point Chauncy appeared as a defender of what he called 'The Good Old Way'.

During his summer in Boston, Davenport had specifically sought out Chauncy to pronounce judgment on his spiritual state. Their encounter took place in the doorway of Chauncy's study, and Chauncy bluntly told Davenport that he was suffering from 'a heated imagination'. Chauncy subsequently published two major attacks on the revival: *Enthusiasm Described and Cautioned Against* (1742) and *Seasonable Thoughts on the State of Religion in New-England* (1743). Real religion, Chauncy argued in the first, is 'a sober, calm, reasonable thing'. The second work detailed his conviction that human affections were actually base animal passions that needed to be held in check by man's more noble faculty—reason.

'If such things are enthusiasm'

In response to such attacks as those of Chauncy, Edwards wrote two powerful defences of the revival: *The Distinguishing Marks of a Work of the Spirit of*

God (1741) and *Some Thoughts concerning the present Revival of Religion in New-England* (1743). In the second of these works he actually documented some experiences that his wife Sarah had gone through from 1735 onwards but especially in January and February 1742— though without naming Sarah or giving any indication that he was speaking about his wife.

Her husband records that Sarah was given, 'such views of the glory of the divine perfections and Christ's excellencies', that her soul was 'swallowed up with light and love...that was altogether unspeakable'. Sometimes such experiences lasted 'for five or six hours together' with a clear

Above: This rock marks the site where the meeting house stood in which Jonathan Edwards preached his famous sermon Sinners in the Hands of an Angry God, *opening the windows of heaven to revival in Enfield*

Below: This house, possibly the old parsonage, stands beside the site of the meeting house

sense of 'the infinite beauty...of Christ's person, and the heavenly sweetness of his transcendent love'. The result was that her 'heart was swallowed up in a kind of glow of Christ's love, coming down from Christ's heart in heaven, as a constant stream of

'Sinners in the Hands of an Angry God'

On 8 July, 1741, at the Congregationalist church in Enfield, Connecticut, Jonathan Edwards delivered what is probably the most famous and controversial sermon in American history: 'Sinners in the Hands of an Angry God'. The members of the congregation at Enfield appear to have been oblivious to the revival that was going on in nearby towns such as Suffield. But the response that Sunday was dramatic. Before Edwards had finished preaching on Deuteronomy 32:35 ('their foot shall slip in due time'), there was a 'great moaning and crying out'. As Edwards' words sunk in, people cried out for mercy and asked what they had to do to be saved.

Though not an over emotional discourse, Edwards, like other great preachers of the revival, minced no words when it came to sin. 'Every unconverted man properly belongs to hell,' he told the congregation that morning, and there is 'nothing that keeps wicked men at any one moment out of hell, but the mere pleasure of God.' He wanted his hearers to reflect seriously on the horrors of hell. Taking phrases like 'the fierceness and wrath of God' from Revelation 19:15 for example, he said, 'Oh, how dreadful must that be! Who can utter or conceive what such expressions carry in them!'

He urged upon his hearers the truth that those who have no interest in Jesus, the only mediator between God and fallen humanity, have absolutely 'nothing to lay hold of to save themselves' and 'nothing to keep off the flames of wrath'. Edwards compared the sinner who ignored the mercy of God to 'a spider, or some loathsome insect' being held over a fire in a fireplace. Just so is the sinner in danger every day of being plunged into hell. All who have 'never passed under a great change of heart, by the mighty power of the Spirit of God' are under God's wrath—they 'are in the hands of an angry God'.

This sermon is not at all a typical Edwards sermon. It is an 'awakening sermon', designed to rouse men and women, and even children, out of the spiritual slumber of sin. The goal of the sermon, preached from a heart of love, was to make the hearer see and feel the horror of being damned and to flee to Christ.

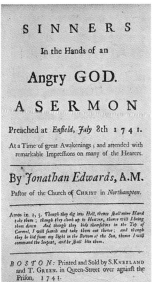

Above: *Front page of* Sinners in the Hands of an Angry God

Above: The interior of the Old South
Meeting House in Newburyport, MA

sweet light'. On other occasions,
it was 'an extraordinary sense of
the awful majesty and greatness
of God', a sense of his holiness
'as of a flame infinitely pure and
bright' and 'an extraordinary
view of the infinite terribleness of
the wrath of God'. Accompanying
these experiences were a number
of unusual bodily phenomena.
Edwards told his readers that
the 'views of divine things' that
Sarah was given, often caused her
body to lose 'all ability to stand
or speak.' At other times she was
filled with such overpowering
joy that she had 'to leap with all
the might, with joy and mighty
exultation of soul'.

Edwards emphasized that
Sarah's experiences were
accompanied by 'an increase
of humility and meekness'
and 'a great alteration' for
the better with regard to her
former weaknesses and failings.

Without the presence of these
God-centred virtues, the physical
manifestations would have been
of absolutely no value. Edwards
concluded his account of Sarah's
experience: 'Now if such things
are enthusiasm, and the fruits of a
distempered brain, let my brain be
evermore possessed of that happy
distemper!'

The Religious Affections

By the time Edwards published
The Religious Affections, the
religious situation in New
England was increasingly
polarized between those who
sided with Chauncy's rationalism
and those who were prepared
to defend men like Davenport,
excesses and all. A third work by
Edwards, *A Treatise Concerning
the Religious Affections* (1746),
sought to carve out a biblical
middle way between these
extremes (see picture page 113).

To the 'zealots' like
Davenport, Edwards stressed that
biblical Christianity must involve
the mind and reason because

Above: A view of Newburyport from the steeple of the Old South Meeting House, overlooking the Merrimack river

when God converts a person, light is shed upon the mind. On the other hand, there is much more to conversion than enlightenment. In response to rationalists like Chauncy, Edwards maintained that genuine spirituality flows out from a heart aflame with the love of God. There is no genuine Christianity without a warmed heart. It is vital to note that the longest section of the book is a reply to Davenport. Edwards obviously regarded the misguided zeal of a Davenport as a much more serious hindrance to the advance of the gospel in times of revival than the rationalism of a Chauncy.

However, the work is also the fruit of Edwards' careful thought since his conversion on a question that had been central to the Puritan vision: What is a truly biblical spirituality like? Edwards outlined twelve marks of such a spirituality. Among them were a love for God as he is in himself, humility, Christ-like gentleness, an insatiable longing for more of

God and finally, good works.

To this twelfth and final sign Edwards devotes more space than to any of the others, a fact that indicates that it loomed largest in his mind. True spirituality bears visible fruit in Christian practice and living in the world. The real believer makes Christianity his main business not only on Sundays, but that 'business which he perseveres in…as long as he lives'. In other words, a zeal for 'good works, good fruits' are to be taken as sure evidence that a person possesses 'a true principle of grace'.

Not without just cause has this book, *A Treatise Concerning the Religious Affections,* been considered one of the richest books on Christian spirituality in the history of the church.

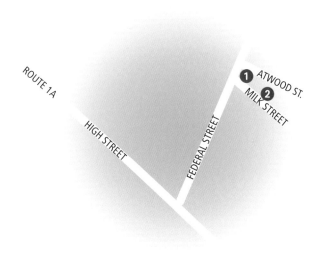

ROUTE 1A

① ATWOOD ST.

② MILK STREET

HIGH STREET

FEDERAL STREET

NEWBURYPORT MA

1 OLD SOUTH CHURCH   2 OLD PARSONAGE

TRAVEL INFORMATION

Below: Boston Common

Newburyport, MA

Newburyport is an old New England seafaring community with many beautiful homes from the late colonial and early Republic periods. General information is available from the Chamber of Commerce website.

Old South Presbyterian Church (Meeting House), Newburyport, MA

29 Federal St, Newburyport, MA. ☎ 978–465–9666. Old South was built in 1756 as a direct result of the Great Awakening. It is a wonderful example of mid-

eighteenth century church architecture. The church has done much in the last few years to enhance its historic past. George Whitefield preached his last sermon in the parsonage of this church and is buried under the pulpit in a crypt which is still available to the general public to this day. They also have a desk that belonged to Whitefield. For tours of the church you will need to contact them directly as they do not have regularly scheduled hours. They welcome the tours but suggest a modest donation. Their website also includes a map and directions to the church.

Above: *Painting of the First Presbyterian Society Old South Meeting House as it was in the time of Whitefield*

Enfield, Connecticut

Jonathan Edwards preached his famous sermon: 'Sinners in the Hands of an Angry God', at the meeting house in Enfield, CT. The meeting house no longer stands but an engraved stone now marks the spot of this historic sermon. It is located at the entrance to the Montessori School, 1370 Enfield Street (Route 5), Enfield, CT 06082.

Additional historic Enfield information can be obtained from The Enfield Historical Society, Inc.

1294 Enfield Street (Route 5) P.O. Box 587, Enfield, CT 06083. ☎ 860–745–1729. Check their website.

⑥ A sorrowful, strange affair

It seems incredible that such a fruitful ministry as that of Edwards in Northampton could end unhappily, but such was the case when the congregation voted to dismiss him as their pastor

During the time of the Great Awakening, we are told that Edwards' Northampton parsonage was constantly 'thronged with persons' who had come to 'lay open their spiritual concerns' to Edwards and 'seek his advice and direction'. Adding to this throng were students who came to be mentored by Edwards. The first was probably Joseph Bellamy, who graduated from Yale in 1735 and who studied with Edwards throughout 1736. He subsequently became a pastor in Bethlehem, Connecticut, in 1740 when he was only twenty. He would become, in Edwards' words, 'one of my most intimate friends' and was the recipient of more extant letters from Edwards than any other correspondent. Edwards would also write a recommendatory preface to Bellamy's influential book *True Religion Delineated*, when it appeared in 1750.

Another student was Samuel Hopkins. He was a senior student at Yale in 1741 when he heard Edwards deliver the commencement sermon that year that would form the heart of *The Distinguishing Marks of a Work of the Spirit of God*. Hopkins immediately decided that here was the man under whom he

wished to pursue further studies. Without any advance warning he turned up on the front step of the Edwards household in December of that year. The man with whom he had come to study was away on a preaching tour. However, Sarah was used to such visitors and invited Hopkins to stay for the winter. Over the following year and a half Hopkins had three extensive stays in the Edwards' home. He not only became Edwards' first biographer—his memoir was published in 1765—

Above: *First Church of Bethlehem, Connecticut*

Facing page: *Joseph Bellamy's house, now The Bellamy-Ferriday House and Garden Archives in Bethlehem Connecticut (see page 89)*

but a leading interpreter of his thought in the latter half of the eighteenth century.

Two deaths in the family

Another young man whom Edwards helped was David Brainerd. Unlike Bellamy and Hopkins, Edwards did not really mentor Brainerd, but Brainerd turned to him for help on two important occasions. The first was in the autumn of 1743. Brainerd had been expelled from Yale during his second year for imprudent remarks about the spirituality of one of his tutors. Edwards appears to have met Brainerd in the autumn of 1743 and sought to get him reinstated at Yale, but to no avail.

The second occasion occurred in May of 1747. After an intense period of mission work among North American Indians in western Massachusetts, Pennsylvania, and New Jersey, Brainerd, his body wracked with tuberculosis, made his way to Northampton. The Edwards family already had one sick young minister in their home, Eleazar Wheelock. Moreover, only a few weeks before Brainerd's arrival, Sarah had given birth to their eighth daughter, Elizabeth. It says much for Sarah's resilient strength

Above: *Portrait of Samuel Hopkins in the Congregational Library, Boston*

Left: *Samuel Hopkins' home in Newport, Rhode Island, where he spent the later years of his pastoral life not only as a major interpreter of Edwards' thought but as an avowed abolitionist. His church in Newport became the first in America to exclude slave owners from membership*

Above: *First Congregational Church, Newport where Samuel Hopkins made slave owning a disqualification for membership*

Left: *Samuel Hopkins' grave sits aside the First Congregational Church of Newport, Rhode Island*

that she willingly accepted the burden of the young missionary's care.

Initially there were some hopes for Brainerd's recovery, just as Wheelock had recovered. But writing to Joseph Bellamy in September, Edwards told his friend that, 'Mr. Brainerd is now at my house, and has been here a long time, in a very low state, growing weaker and weaker; he is like to be here till he dies.' Brainerd died on 9 October 1747. Though he was only twenty-nine, the young man had made a deep impression on Edwards, and by December Edwards had determined to write a memoir of Brainerd. Putting aside other pressing literary projects, he poured himself into writing what turned out to be an outstanding literary success. Published in Boston in early 1749, it has been in print ever since.

While Edwards did not overlook Brainerd's failings, in particular, his tendency to melancholy, he did see in Brainerd a model of the piety he had so earnestly recommended in his own *Religious Affections*. Brainerd was a man, in Edwards' words: 'who had indeed sold all for Christ and had entirely

Above: A view of the Connecticut river in Haddam Connecticut, the birth place of David Brainerd

Left: The plaque that marks the birth place of David Brainerd, 20 April 1718 in Haddam, Connecticut

devoted himself to God, and made his glory his highest end.' His devotion to God was what true revival always produced, one imbued with a love for missionary work, determined loyalty to Christian orthodoxy, indefatigable courage, and zeal for good works. His was 'a religion… like the steady lights of heaven; that are constant principles of light, though sometimes hid with clouds.'

Just over four months after the death of Brainerd, another death occurred in the Edwards household. Seventeen-year old Jerusha Edwards, who had been Brainerd's nurse through the entire time of his illness, died of a fever on Sunday 14 February. Edwards was grief-stricken. It was, he told Joseph Bellamy, 'our sore affliction'. His shock may have been in part because she had been ill for only five days before her death. Edwards told one of his Scottish correspondents, John Erskine, that Jerusha was 'the flower of the family' and that her

One of the few surviving letters from Jonathan to his wife was written when Sarah was away in Boston during the summer of 1748. After telling Sarah about a variety of domestic matters, Jonathan exclaimed, 'We have been without you as long as we know how to be'! Obviously he had come to the point where he was feeling absolutely overwhelmed by the running of their house.

In fact, Samuel Hopkins specified that Jonathan left the actual temporal matters of their home 'almost entirely to Mrs. Edwards, who was better able than most of her sex to take the whole care of them on her hands.' So Sarah had to supervise, for example, such domestic matters as the cooking and preparation of all the meals along with home industries like the carding and spinning of wool. She also had the responsibility of such regular outdoor activities as the cultivation and

care of a garden plot that came with the parsonage, the milking of their cows, and the harvesting and storage of hay for their cows' winter feed. As 'a good economist', Hopkins noted that Sarah hated waste: 'that nothing be lost' was with her a key maxim for running a godly home. In addition to all of this, there was the raising of their eleven children in such a way that 'they might be born of God by having Christ formed in them', as Hopkins expressed it.

death was a 'great loss'. What comforted him and his family was that she was 'a very eminent saint' and there had been 'remarkable appearances of piety' in her life from childhood. Jerusha was buried beside Brainerd in the Northampton cemetery, where today their bodies still lie awaiting the resurrection. Her nursing of Brainerd and their being buried side by side have given rise to all kinds of romanticising about their being engaged to one another. However, there is no certain evidence of this.

The issue to divide the church

The two years after Jerusha's death were not easy ones for Edwards. On 22 June 1750, he was dismissed as pastor by an overwhelming majority of the male members of the Northampton congregation. The simplest explanation for Edwards'

dismissal is that his attempt to change one of the central aspects of the ministry of his revered

Above: Brainerd rode in all weathers to take the gospel to the Indians

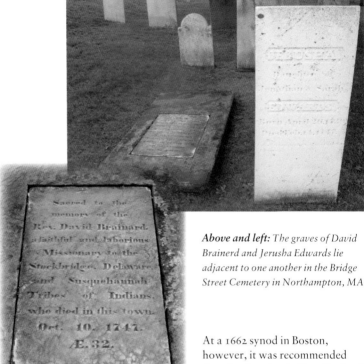

Above and left: The graves of David Brainerd and Jerusha Edwards lie adjacent to one another in the Bridge Street Cemetery in Northampton, MA

Sacred to the memory of the Rev. David Brainard, a faithful and laborious Missionary to the Stockbridge, Delaware and Susquehannah Tribes of Indians who died in this town Oct. 10. 1747. Æ. 32.

At a 1662 synod in Boston, however, it was recommended that the churches in New England adopt what was termed the Half-Way Covenant. This covenant allowed the unregenerate children of believing parents to have their infants baptized provided that these unregenerate adults declared first their belief in the Christian worldview and second their determination to lead a moral life. Participation in the Lord's Supper and voting remained the privilege of those who could profess conversion and thus were full members of the church. It was hoped that those who embraced the Half-Way Covenant would eventually go all the way and become fully fledged members.

It soon became apparent, however, that many of the Half-Way members were quite content

grandfather, Solomon Stoddard, led to a massive backlash in the church, especially from some of his relatives.

In the early days of Puritan New England, many Congregational churches required applicants for membership to give a public testimony of the Lord's dealings with their souls. In addition to living a morally blameless life, anyone wishing to join the congregation as a member had to testify that he or she had indeed become a new creation in Christ. Among the privileges of membership were access to baptism for one's children and participation in the Lord's Supper.

to be such and had no intention of making a confession of faith to become full members. Solomon Stoddard, who had inherited a bent towards individualism from his mother, felt that a different approach was desperately needed. He himself had received assurance of salvation while coming to the Lord's Table in the spring of 1672. Thus, he began to argue that at the Lord's Supper 'in a special manner, Christ would be present to reveal himself, in all his fullness of love to the souls of men.' In the strong expectation that the Lord's Table could become a place of conversion, he was willing to admit to the Table all who professed a willingness to follow the teaching of Scripture and whose outward lives were morally unobjectionable. As Stoddard declared in a sermon: 'The Lord's Supper is appointed … for the begetting of grace as well as for the strengthening of grace.'

Stoddard's position did not go unopposed. Among his strongest opponents in Boston were Increase

Above: *Brainerd preaching among the Susquehanna Indians of the Delaware River*

Below and left: *Edward Taylor's gravestone and that of his wife Elizabeth beside the first Church in Westfield, Massachusetts*

ORIGINAL TOMBSTONES
OF
REV. EDWARD TAYLOR
AND HIS WIFE
ELIZABETH
HE WAS OUR FIRST PASTOR AND
THE FIRST GREAT AMERICAN POET

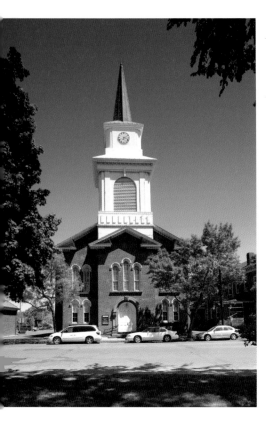

Left: The First
Congregational Church in
Westfield, Massachusetts

Below right: Cotton
Mather, the influential
New England Puritan

Joseph Bellamy. As he studied Scripture, Edwards found that the Lord's Table was a place where faith is sealed, not begun as his grandfather had maintained. Furthermore, Edwards was concerned that Stoddard's practice in the Northampton church allowed unconverted people to assume that good morals and intellectual affirmation of Christian doctrine were sufficient to be right with God, when, in fact, what was needed was the new birth. In other words, Edwards came to believe that Stoddard's long-time opponents, the Mathers, were right after all. By 1746, it appears, his mind had been made up, but it was to be another two years before he made his views public to his congregation.

Mathers and his son Cotton, and the Puritan poet Edward Taylor in Westfield, Massachusetts, not far from Stoddard in Northampton. Cotton Mather bluntly declared Stoddard's dogma 'to be a new thing' in the history of the church. Eventually, however, many in western Massachusetts were won over to what may be described as Stoddardeanism.

Publicly, admission to the Lord's Table does not appear to have been an issue for Jonathan Edwards until the late 1740s. But there is little doubt that he had wrestled with the issue for a long time, initially relating his doubts about Stoddardeanism only to his wife and close friends like

Edwards must have had a good inkling of how things would unfold, but he persevered because he was a man of firm principle; once he was convinced that a theological position was mandated by Scripture, he would not give in. Therefore when, in December of 1748, a young man came forward to join the congregation, Edwards declared that he must profess to be regenerate before he would be allowed to become a member of the church. The man was a professing believer, but when he realized that the manner of his joining the church would place him at the heart of a brewing controversy he told Edwards he was unwilling to pursue coming into membership. In taking this position, Edwards found himself opposed by most of his congregation, as he made clear in a letter he wrote in May 1749 to the Scottish Presbyterian minister John Erskine. He told Erskine: 'A very great difficulty has arisen between me and my people, relating to qualifications for communion at the Lord's table.' After outlining his grandfather's views and then his own position, Edwards commented, 'I know not but this affair will issue in a separation between me and my people.'

Criticisms of Edwards

As with any controversy, other issues were brought into the fray. In the spring of 1744, there had been a discipline case that Edwards had handled somewhat poorly. Some young men in their twenties had obtained a textbook on midwifery and used its contents

to make lewd remarks to young women in the town. Part of Edwards' response was to read to the congregation one Sunday morning after worship a list of various young men with whom he and a number of the church leaders wished to talk about this matter. But Edwards failed to distinguish between those who were among the accused and those who were just witnesses. Not surprisingly, he deeply offended some of the parents of those who were innocent of the charge.

There was also the complaint that Edwards had failed to regularly visit his congregation. Samuel Hopkins later defended him by saying that it appeared to Edwards that 'he could do the greatest good to souls and most promote the interest of Christ by preaching and writing, and conversing with persons under religious impressions in his study' where, according to Hopkins, he would spend thirteen hours a day. Edwards' salary— admitted by himself to be one of the largest ministerial salaries outside of Boston— was also brought into the dispute. He and his family were criticized, in his words, for their 'manner of spending' and 'the clothes that [they] wore'. In this regard, Edwards defended himself by rightly arguing that he had such a large family to take care of, and his home, by reason of all the people he had to entertain, was something of an inn. It is noteworthy that when George Whitefield had visited the Edwards household in October 1740, he noted that the Edwards children were 'not dressed in silks and satins, but plain, as become the children of those who, in all things, ought to be examples of Christian simplicity.'

However the central issue had to do with what Edwards described as 'the qualifications necessary for admission to the privileges of members'. Typically Edwards sought to explain his

Below: The grave of Joseph Hawley III in the Bridge Street Cemetery in Northampton. Hawley was a cousin to Edwards and a major opponent during the communion controversy. Hawley would later in life repent of his involvement in Edwards' dismissal. He became a much respected patriot of the revolution

views in print with a book: *An Humble Inquiry into the Rules of the Word of God concerning the Qualifications requisite to a Complete Standing and Full Communion in the Visible Christian Church* (1749). He urged his congregation to read the work, but few did so. Two of those who did read the book were cousins of Edwards: Elisha Williams, who had once been Rector of Yale and Edwards' tutor at Yale, and his brother Solomon. Elisha was highly regarded as a theologian and his reply, eagerly anticipated by Edwards' opponents in Northampton, was never written; it was Solomon who eventually responded to Edwards' book. It is noteworthy that their opposition to Edwards was typical of most of Edwards' cousins who bore the surname of Williams. The Williams clan was a powerful group that controlled much of the commerce up and down the Connecticut River and they proved to be formidable enemies.

Above: *The tomb on the left is that of Thomas Clap in the Grove Street Cemetery, New Haven, CT. Clap was the rector of Yale when David Brainerd was expelled*

During the controversy, and especially in the actual week of his dismissal, Edwards displayed remarkable calmness. One contemporary noted that Edwards 'appeared like a man of God, whose happiness was out of reach of his enemies, and whose treasure was not only a future but a present good, overbalancing all imaginable ills of life.'

'Thrown upon the wide ocean of the world'

The congregational vote for Edwards' dismissal took place on 22 June, when the vast majority of the 230 male members consented to his dismissal. Nine days later, on 1 July 1750, Edwards gave his farewell sermon. In some ways, he did not spare his hearers that day. 'A contentious people,' he warned them, 'will be a miserable people'. The 'contention, heat of spirit, evil speaking' that Edwards had experienced during the controversy, he said plainly, are 'directly contrary to the spirit of Christianity'. As he had said on another occasion many years before: 'a contentious man and a Christian' are as different as 'light and darkness'. There was little doubt in Edwards' mind that Northampton was a remarkably 'contentious town'.

Yet, Edwards stressed that he bore the people of the town no ill-will. He urged those who had supported him, some of whom wanted to form a new congregation in the town, to 'avoid all bitterness towards others' and to 'maintain, with great diligence and watchfulness, a Christian meekness and sedateness of spirit'. He admonished them to 'seek the prosperity of this town: and never think you behave yourselves as becomes Christians, but when you sincerely, sensibly and fervently

Above: Ezra Stiles home, Newport

love all men of whatever party or opinion.'

With no fixed salary, the Edwards family now found itself in a situation of enormous financial strain. Another child, Pierpont, had been born only three months before. At forty-six years of age, Edwards was certainly not old by our standards, but from his perspective he was, and his options were thus quite limited. Moreover, he was very conscious that he had no other skills but those of a preacher. As he said, 'I am fitted for no other business but study.'

Some of his Scottish friends offered to secure him a position in Scotland, and, unknown to Edwards, Presbyterians in Virginia were also organizing an effort to bring him there; they had even obtained pledges of financial support for him. But by the time this news reached him, he had already made other plans. He had accepted a call to a mission station at Stockbridge—on the very edge of the frontier.

Four days after his farewell sermon, Edwards had told John Erskine: 'I am now as it were thrown upon the wide ocean of the world, and know not what will become of me and my numerous family.' Yet, he was not prepared to give way to despair. As he went on, 'We are in the hands of God, and I bless him. I am not anxious concerning his disposal of us. I hope I shall not distrust him, nor be unwilling to submit to his will. And I have cause of thankfulness, that there seems also to be such a disposition in my family.'

TRAVEL INFORMATION

Newport, Rhode Island

Newport, Rohde Island contains many
historic homes and sites. In addition
to the rich colonial and early American
history of Newport, it is famous for the
many large mansions built by families like
the Vanderbilts.

Both Samuel Hopkins (Edwards'
student) and Ezra Stiles (later president
of Yale) pastored churches in this town.
Hopkins pastored what is now the
Newport Congregational Church.

Newport Congregational Church

73 Pelham Street, Newport, Rhode Island
02840.

Samuel Hopkins is buried beside the
church.

Ezra Stiles House

14 Clarke Street, Newport, Rhode Island.

Samuel Hopkins House

16 Division Street, Newport, Rhode
Island.

Much additional information on the
historic houses and mansions of Newport
can be obtained from Newport Historical
Society.

Newport Historical Society

82 Tuoro Street, Newport, Rhode Island
02840. ☎ 401–846–0813.

Newport Mansions

424 Bellevue Avenue, Newport, Rhode
Island 02840. ☎ 401–847–1000.

Bethlehem, Connecticut

Joseph Bellamy, a prominent student
of Jonathan Edwards, pastored in
Bethlehem, CT. His house has been
beautifully restored and is the site of The
Bellamy-Ferriday House and Garden. In
addition to its beauty, there are historical
documents housed here relating to
Bellamy. For hours of operation and
directions you should contact them
directly. The First Church is located just
a short distance down Main Street and
contains some of Bellamy's published
writings and his pulpit.

The Bellamy-Ferriday House and garden

9 Main Street North, Bethlehem, CT
06751. ☎ 203–266–7596 (see page 76).

First Church of Bethlehem

21 Main Street South, Bethlehem, CT
06751. ☎ 203–266–7288.

Left: Brainerd preaching to the Susquehanna Indians

❼ Come and enjoy the light

When Edwards' name is mentioned, most think of him as a theologian and preacher. But he was also a missionary who stands at the fountainhead of the modern missionary movement

Edwards preached in Stockbridge for the first three months of 1751 and accepted the call to be the town's minister on 22 February. But he waited until the autumn of that year to move his family there.

The founding of the Stockbridge Mission has its background in both the vision and tragedies of the previous generations of Puritans in New England. When the Massachusetts Bay Colony was established in 1629, missions to the Native Americans were in view. The colony's Charter sought to establish a civil and religious policy for the English settlers so that 'their good life and orderly conversation may win and incite the natives of the Country to the knowledge and obedience of the only true God and Saviour of mankind and the Christian Faith, which … is the principal end of this plantation.'

This vision was partially pursued over the following years most notably by the pastor of the church in Roxbury, John Eliot, who died in his eighty-sixth year in 1690. His missionary endeavours won him the title of Apostle to the Indians and his labours included translating the Bible into the language of the Massachusett Indians.

In the congregation that Eliot pastored at Roxbury there was a young man who, over his lifetime, would have numerous encounters with the Native Americans of New England. John Williams became the minister of the church in Deerfield, Massachusetts, only a few miles north of Northampton, in 1686. The following year he married Eunice Mather, the daughter of the first minister of Northampton, Eleazar

Above: *The marker erected for the Stockbridge Indians buried in the Stockbridge cemetery. This marker names only two Stockbridge Indians: one of them, Capt. John Konkapot was very prominent in Edwards' day*

Facing page: *Indian monument in Stockbridge, Massachusetts*

John Eliot, Apostle to the Indians

John Eliot, widely loved in his own day for his godly life and character, is chiefly remembered for his ministry among the Indians of eastern Massachusetts. While assistant pastor of the Congregational Church in Roxbury, Massachusetts, Eliot began to preach to the Massachuset Indians in the autumn of 1646. His first sermons were in English and he soon realized the desirability of reaching the Indians in their own tongue. He therefore commenced study of the Massachuset dialect of coastal Algonquian and in time became extremely proficient as both a speaker and author in the language. Between 1654 and 1688, Eliot produced at least twenty different books in Massachuset, including some Puritan classics, and his translation of the Bible (1661–1663) was the first Bible to be printed in North America.

Eliot helped to establish fourteen communities of what were called 'praying Indians', that is, Indian Christians. By 1674 there were around 1100 Massachuset Indians in these villages with about twenty-four ordained Indian pastors. Sadly, Eliot's labours were largely nullified by King Philip's War in 1675–1676, in which the Puritan colonists found themselves at war with the native Americans. Compared to the size of the population, it was the bloodiest war in American history and sowed deep distrust between the English and the Indians. Only four of Eliot's villages of 'praying Indians' survived, and these eventually dwindled away. By the nineteenth century there were no native speakers who could read Eliot's Bible. That Bible, though, remains as the symbol of a remarkable ministry.

Above: Monument to John Eliot in Roxbury Massachusetts

Below: The current building of the church John Eliot pastored, the First Church of Roxbury at John Eliot Square, Roxbury Massachusetts

Mather, brother of Increase Mather. Her father died when she was a child and her mother married the second minister of Northampton, Solomon Stoddard. Thus Eunice was a stepsister to Jonathan Edwards' mother Esther.

The Deerfield massacre

For much of the 18th century France and Great Britain were at war, struggling for world domination. One of the wars between these two European powers lasted from 1702 to 1713 and is known to history as Queen Anne's War. The English settlers became concerned, and rightly so, that the French would use native Indians to raid English settlements on the American frontier. Deerfield was just such a settlement. On a cold February morning in 1704, a band of Indians, who had come down from Canada at the urging of the French, attacked and destroyed Deerfield, taking over 100 captives.

Among the thirty-nine settlers killed were two of John and Eunice Williams' younger children, six week-old Jerusha and six year-old John. John, Eunice, and five of their children were force-marched by their captors to Canada. Eunice, weak from recent childbirth and distraught from the tragedy, was tomahawked on the second day of the march. All of the remaining Williams family would eventually be released over the next few years except the youngest girl Eunice,

Below and left: The monument in the Deerfield Cemetery over the mound of the mass burial of the victims of the Deerfield massacre of 1704

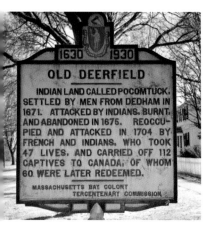

Left: Marker in the Deerfield Massachusetts cemetery for the mass grave for those killed in the Deerfield Massacre, 1704

Jonathan Edwards was only a few months old when the Deerfield raid and massacre took place, but the horrors of that night stayed long in the hearts and minds of his parents. When another sister was born to Jonathan in 1705 they named her Eunice. It was also during this war that Jonathan's own father, Timothy Edwards, was enlisted to serve as chaplain to the troops. Severe ill health precluded him from travelling with them farther than Albany, New York. There he was released from service, and because he was so ill he had to be taken back home in a wagon. Thirty-five years later,

who remained in Canada for the rest of her life and eventually married an Indian there and became a Roman Catholic. The account of the raid and trials of the captivity were chronicled in a work by John Williams after his return. Entitled *The Redeemed Captive, Returning to Zion*, it became something of a bestseller.

Above: The Deerfield River in February. The captives were taken across this river on 29 February 1703 as they were force marched to Canada by the French and Indians

in the summer of 1740, Eunice Williams came with François Xavier Aronsen, her Mohawk husband, to visit her family in Massachusetts. Edwards was there on the occasion and preached a sermon, hoping against hope that his distant cousin might renounce her adherence to Roman Catholicism and stay with her family. But it was not to be. Eunice and her Mohawk husband returned to Canada.

Queen Anne's War ended in 1713 and in the years that followed only a minimal amount of effort was expended by the settlers in evangelizing the natives. Solomon Stoddard was deeply troubled by this and in the last of his published works he chided New Englanders for their lack of interest in missions to the natives. Entitled *Question Whether God is not Angry with the Country for Doing so Little Towards the Conversion of the Indians* (1723), the work argued that New England's failure to preach the gospel to the Native Americans was the reason that God had punished them with war and pestilence. Seven years later, in 1730, the Royal Governor of Massachusetts, Jonathan Belcher, expressed a desire to see mission work grow amongst the natives and to this end he proposed the establishment of a settlement for the specific purpose of evangelism.

Below: John Sergeant, first missionary to the Stockbridge Indians

The Stockbridge mission

Belcher's proposal became a reality between 1736 and 1739 when, upon the request of some Mahicans (also called Mohican, Housatonic or Stockbridge Indians) to have a missionary settle among them and teach them the gospel, a mission was established on the Housatonic River in the western frontier of Massachusetts. During the previous century the Mahicans had been a significant tribe who ranged over the land between the Hudson and Connecticut Rivers and as far north as Lakes George and Champlain. But long and bloody conflicts with other Native Americans had severely reduced their nation and now they needed the protection of the British.

John Sergeant, a young graduate from Yale, was formally ordained to the mission work there. Over the next ten years Sergeant enjoyed some success in reaching the Mahicans through a school that he started as well as through the church. His missionary efforts, though, were blunted somewhat by his embrace of some theologically liberal convictions. Sadly Sergeant was taken ill and died in 1749. Edwards judged that the change in Sergeant came after his marriage to one of the Williams clan, Abigail Williams. Abigail was a gifted woman, whose temperament, in Edwards' opinion, was disposed 'much more to dominion than subjection' and she seems to have ruled the marriage.

By the spring of 1750, Abigail, and her father, Ephraim Williams—the brother of William Williams of Hatfield, who was Edwards' uncle and who had preached the sermon at Solomon Stoddard's funeral—thought they had found a replacement for John Sergeant in another Yale graduate, Ezra Stiles.

Stiles would later become a stalwart Calvinist and a President of Yale, but at this stage in his life he was consumed with doubts about even the most basic Christian beliefs. He soon realized

Above: Deerfield Post Office designed after the Third Deerfield Meeting House 1696 to 1728. Edwards would have been familiar with the original

that he was not the man to take charge of a mission station and so the way was clear for Edwards to be considered for the position. This must have been a shock for Abigail and her father, who shared the general dislike by the Williams clan for Jonathan Edwards!

What is interesting is that when Abigail Williams actually met Edwards she would admit, in a letter written to Stiles in February 1751, that the new minister of Stockbridge had 'conducted [himself] with wisdom and prudence … He is learned, polite, and free in conversation, and more catholic [open-minded] than I had supposed.' Others of the Williams clan based in Stockbridge were not so generous. Abigail's half-brother Ephraim Jr. viewed Edwards as unsociable and 'a very great bigot'. Moreover, he was convinced that Edwards did not have a practical bone in his body. 'I am sorry,' he wrote to a cousin-in-law, 'that a head so full of divinity should be so empty of politics.'

The Edwards family made the forty-mile trip to Stockbridge in October. By then two of Edwards' daughters had married. Sarah married Elihu Parsons in June of 1750 and five months later Mary married Timothy Dwight, the son of one of Edwards' strongest supporters in Northampton. The Dwights chose to remain in the town after the family left in 1751. It could not have been easy for Mary to remain in a church that had been so antagonistic to her father. Within a year a third daughter, Esther, had also wed.

Timothy Dwight

Timothy Dwight, the son of Timothy and Mary Dwight, was born in Northampton, Massachusetts. Amazingly precocious, Dwight entered Yale College at the age of thirteen, graduating in 1769. Between 1778 and 1783 he studied theology with his uncle, Jonathan Edwards, Jr. During his pastorate at the Congregational church at Greenfield Hill, Connecticut, he became famous throughout New England for his preaching and for the superb private school that he established close to his church. In 1795, when the presidency of Yale College became vacant, Dwight consented to

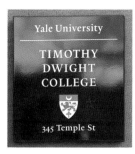

Above: *Plaque on Timothy Dwight College,* Yale *University,* New Haven *CT*

accept this prestigious position and was inaugurated later that same year. During his term of service the College experienced four distinct periods of spiritual awakening. His Yale chapel sermons were published as the five volume *Theology Explained and Defended* (1818–1819); which went through no less than twelve editions in the United States alone. It was Dwight who made what has become a famous remark often attributed to others: ' All that I am and all that I shall be, I owe to my mother.'

EDWARDS'S HOME AT STOCKBRIDGE.

Above: *A print of the Edwards' Stockbridge home from Harper's New Monthly Magazine*

She married the elder Aaron Burr, the President of the fledgling College of New Jersey, which, at the time, was based in Newark. Burr would supervise the move of the college to Princeton in November, 1756, but he did not live long to lead the school in its new location. He died at the age of forty-one in September 1757.

Above: This sundial marks the spot on Main Street in Stockbridge where the Edwards' home once stood

Below: The panels that make up the platform of the pulpit of the First Church in Stockbridge were made from wood taken from the Edwards' house when it was demolished

The first home that the Edwards family occupied had been the home of John Sergeant prior to his marriage. It was in the town and among the Indians.

Sergeant himself, after his marriage to Abigail Williams, had vacated the house for a larger home on Prospect Hill, overlooking the town that was more suitable to the aristocratic tastes of Abigail. This house now sits at the corners of Main Street and Sergeant Street.

The home in which the Edwards family lived has been long gone, though its location is marked today by a sundial. By living among the Indians, Edwards was clearly making a statement that he had genuinely come to minister to these people. It is noteworthy that his son

Above: The Mission House—John and Abigail Sergeant's home still stands as a museum in Stockbridge, Massachusetts

Right: The modern building of the First Church in Stockbridge where John Sergeant was the first minister and Jonathan Edwards the second

Jonathan Jr. would later recall that his boyhood friends were all Indians and that he never spoke English outside of the family circle.

In spite of the hardships that the family faced in relocating to Stockbridge, Edwards could tell his parents in January 1752 that his family had come to like Stockbridge 'far better than they expected'. In particular, he continued, the peace that they enjoyed in Stockbridge was a welcome relief from the tension that had marked the final years in Northampton. In addition, Edwards noted with some pleasure: 'The Indians seem much pleased with my family, especially my wife.'

What prompted Edwards to settle in such a small out-of-the-way frontier village? Some have surmised that Edwards settled here because the rigours of ministry among a smaller congregation would prove minimal, and he could devote himself largely to his study and the major treatises that he wrote during his time in Stockbridge. In other words, some have viewed Edwards in Stockbridge almost like an academic scholar on an extended sabbatical. Samuel Hopkins, in his memoir of his mentor, seems to imply something like this when he states that God gave Edwards 'a quiet retreat' at Stockbridge where he could pursue his writing. This view has been furthered by the belief that Edwards simply preached rehashed sermons from his Northampton years.

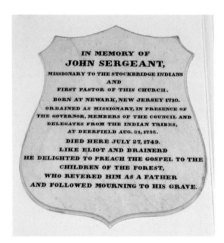

Left and below left:
The marble plaques
commemorating the first two
ministers of the First Church
of Stockbridge

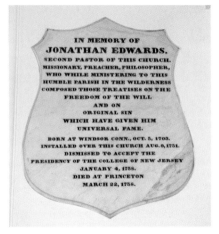

While we cannot say for certain—Edwards himself does not lay out the reasons explicitly—there are several hints within his work and publications from the Northampton years. These include his heart for evangelical revival and genuine and heartfelt conversions. In particular, he had maintained an interest in the success of the Stockbridge mission over the years and had persuaded his Northampton congregation to heavily support the work during the 1740s. There was also a great desire to see the coming of the kingdom of Christ in ever greater manifestations until the Jews are won to Christ en masse, the millennium dawns and the antichrist falls —which like many Protestants of his day he regarded as the Papacy. And in this great advance of the gospel the conversion of the peoples of North America had its place. Nor can we discount the impact of the life of David Brainerd upon Edwards as he edited and published the life and Diary of this eminent example of genuine evangelical spirituality.

Edwards' large correspondence from this period of his life, however, reveals that his pre-eminent goal was to reach the Native Americans with the life-giving gospel. His sermons from this period also show that the largest part were not repeats of Northampton sermons but new sermons constructed with careful attention to the audience to whom they were to be preached and the end to which they were intended. So what may have moved him to take this small obscure charge?

Preaching to the Mohawks

Clear evidence that Edwards' missionary life in Stockbridge has not been appreciated is the fact that up until 1999 not one of the sermons that he preached to the Stockbridge Indians had been published. A number of these sermons are now available in a volume of Edwards' sermons covering the years 1743 to 1758, volume 25 in the twenty-six volume critical edition of Edwards' works published by Yale University Press. They reveal Edwards as a missionary preacher who was able to communicate plainly and effectively in his new evangelistic sphere.

An example of this is a sermon that he delivered to a group of Mohawks on 16 August 1751. A large number of the Mohawk chiefs had come to Albany, New York, to discuss sending their children to the school in Stockbridge. After the discussions, Edwards was given an opportunity to preach to them. He began by stating that 'when God first made man, he had a

Above: *Drawing of Edwards in the First Church of Stockbridge*

Below: *A view of the Housatonic River in Stockbridge, Massachusetts*

principle of holiness in his heart', like a light shining within him. But then the man sinned against God and he 'lost his holiness'. The light that he had was 'put out' and his mind became full of darkness. The long-term result was idolatry: the worship of heavenly bodies, 'images of gold and silver, brass and iron, wood and stone', animals and even the devil.

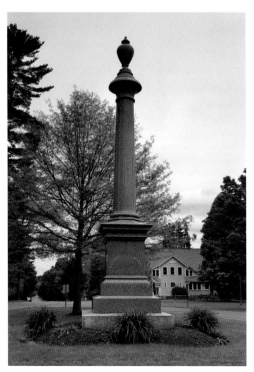

Left: *Edwards Memorial across from the First Church in Stockbridge, erected in 1871 by his descendents*

'they have greatly neglected you', and that neglect was shameful. The 'white people have not behaved like Christians' for if they had, Edwards continued, they would have given the natives the Scriptures and in this way would have shown love for their souls. In fact, many of the 'English and the Dutch' wanted to keep the Natives 'in the dark for the sake of making a gain' of them and their lands. Here Edwards clearly drew upon the thinking of his grandfather Stoddard who had made similar charges nearly thirty years earlier. He also drew upon his long ministry in Northampton where he had been publicly critical of those who lived for material gain, which he believed was positively dangerous to the soul.

But God had mercy on mankind and gave them the Scriptures 'as a light shining in a dark place'. Then Christ came to 'die for sinners' and give further instruction. And so the Bible was completed. Christ gave clear instruction that the Bible and the Gospel were to be taught to all the nations. Those nations that now have the Bible 'enjoy light', while those nations without it 'live in great darkness'. Edwards now spoke plainly: the forefathers of the Mohawk 'have for a great many ages lived in great darkness'. The Europeans, who had the Scriptures and should have taught the Native Americans, have not helped them: 'They have not done their duty to you', he told his hearers,

Edwards then urged his Mohawk hearers: 'Don't content yourselves to live in darkness any longer.' He pleaded, 'We invite you to come and enjoy the light of the Word of God.' If they did, this light would shine into their hearts and change them and make them like Christ, just as 'when you hold a glass out in the light of the sun, the glass will shine with a resemblance of the sun's brightness.'

Though simple in language and structure, this is yet a powerful presentation of the gospel. There is little doubt that this Stockbridge sermon reveals a true missionary heart. Interestingly enough, the whole sermon revolves around the theme of light, which had also dominated his earlier brilliant depiction of the world to come, *Heaven Is a World of Love*. As American historian Ronald Story has expressed it so well, for Edwards: 'light connotes sight and insight, brightness and illumination … something of "sweetness" and even rapture.'

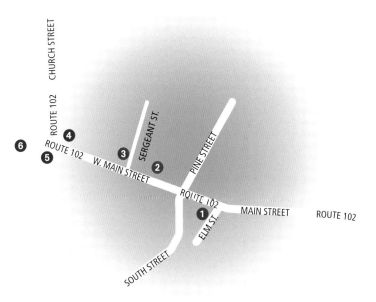

STOCKBRIDGE MA

1 STOCKBRIDGE LIBRARY
2 EDWARDS MEMORIAL
3 MISSION HOUSE
4 STOCKBRIDGE CEMETERY

5 FIRST CONGREGAIONAL CHURCH OF STOCKBRIDGE
6 INDIAN BRUIAL GROUND MONUMENT

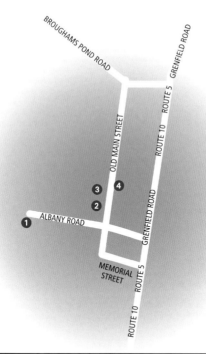

DEERFIELD MA

1 OLD BURIAL GROUND
2 FIRST CHURCH OF DEERFIELD

3 DEERFIELD POST OFFICE
4 VISITOR CENTER

TRAVEL INFORMATION

Stockbridge, MA

Stockbridge is a beautiful New England town nestled in the Berkshires of western Massachusetts. Made popularly famous by Norman Rockwell, the museum which houses many of his paintings is located here. The downtown sector includes a number of quaint shops and eateries and is flanked by the famed Red Lion Inn on one side and the Stockbridge Library on the other. A number of items of interest respecting Edwards can be viewed in The Stockbridge Library Association Historical Collections, housed in the basement of the Library, including portraits of both Jonathan and Sarah Edwards. You will need to contact them directly for hours of operation.

The Stockbridge Library Association Historical Collections

Main Street, Stockbridge MA 01262. ☎ 413–298–5501. They do not yet have a website.

The house built in 1739 by John Sergeant, Stockbridge's first missionary to the local Mohican Indians (not the Mohegans of James Fennimore Cooper fame) still stands and is open for tours. It is a wonderfully preserved example of mid eighteenth century architecture and construction. Sergeant's wife, Abigail, insisted he build the house when they married and she continued to occupy the house after John's death in 1749.

The Mission House Museum and Gardens

19 Main Street, Stockbridge MA 01262. ☎ 413–298–3239.

There is a sundial marking the spot of Edwards' home in Stockbridge in front of the Austen Riggs Center, 25 Main Street, Stockbridge, MA 01262. ☎ 413–298–5511. Edwards was the second pastor of the Congregational Church in Stockbridge.

The First Congregational Church of Stockbridge

4 Main Street Stockbridge, MA 01262. ☎ 413–298–3137.

Across Main Street from the First Congregational Church is the **Stockbridge Cemetery**. There are a number of significant persons buried here, including John Sergeant, first pastor and missionary to the Stockbridge Indians; Timothy and Rhoda Ogden Edwards, son and daughter-in-law of Jonathan and Sarah; Norman Rockwell; Elizabeth Freeman who won her freedom from slavery in 1781 in the famed 'Brom and Bett vs. Ashley' case of Massachusetts; Theodore Sedgwick, her lawyer, whose family plot has descendents buried in concentric circles around him and his wife; and a marker for the Stockbridge Indians who were founding fathers of the church and community.

Next to the Stockbridge Cemetery at the corner of Main Street and Church Street is the **Jonathan Edwards Monument,** placed here in 1871 by the descendents of Jonathan Edwards who met for a famed conference in Stockbridge in 1870. In addition to the monument a memorial volume was published under the title, *The Memorial Volume of the Edwards Family Meeting at Stockbridge, Mass., September 6–7, A.D. 1870.*

Deerfield, MA

Historic Deerfield. 84B Old Main Street, Deerfield, MA 01342. ☎ 413–774–5581.

Deerfield is a richly restored community of the late colonial and early Republic period situated in the beautiful countryside of western Massachusetts north of Northampton. Jonathan Edwards' maternal aunt, Eunice Stoddard Williams, and her two children were victims of the notorious Deerfield Massacre. See page 93. Aside from the many restored houses which can be toured, there is a visitor center and museum that are a wealth of information on this event and the community. The Deerfield cemetery also contains a mass grave for the victims of the massacre and the individual graves of Eunice and Rev. John Williams.

Above: *John Sergeant's grave with his wife Abigail Williams Sergeant Dwight beside him in the cemetery at Stockbridge, Massachusetts*

❽ The legacy of Edwards

The enduring legacy of Edwards is especially found in his massive defence of Calvinism. When people later thought about Edwards after his death they remembered him as both a remarkable theologian and a philosophical genius

Edwards regarded himself as a British subject and New England as part of a transatlantic British society. As such, he was not unconcerned about the struggles of his nation with her inveterate enemy of the 18th century —the Roman Catholic country of France. Due to the proximity of New England to Roman Catholic Canada, the European wars between these two nation states always spilled over onto the North American continent.

The French and Indian War
Armed conflict came again to North America early in 1754 when what was known as the French and Indian War broke out; in Britain this war would be known as the Seven Years' War. In the midst of the early stages of the fighting and the rumours of battles, Edwards fell ill and was essentially away from the pulpit from late July to January, apart from some preaching in September. Edwards told his Scottish correspondent John Erskine in a letter dated April 1755 that it was the 'longest and most tedious sickness' he had ever had and that at one point the sickness had 'exceedingly wasted' his 'flesh and strength' such that

he looked 'like a skeleton'.

On 1 September 1754, though, Edwards had felt well enough to preach. Morning worship had just finished when a man rushed into town with the horrific news that he had come upon an Abenaki Indian from Canada attempting to kidnap a young child from an outlying home. When this Abenaki was seen in the act he tomahawked the child and

Above: A view of Nassau Hall by F Childs published by George Thompson in the mid nineteenth century

Facing page: Nassau Hall, completed in 1756 two years before Edwards died, was constructed with money donated by Governor Jonathan Belcher and comprised the full campus of Princeton University

ran off. The man subsequently discovered another Abenaki in the house. This second Abenaki had killed an infant and servant and was about to attack the father of the house and two other little boys. The Abenaki also ran off when the man providentially appeared. News of the killings ran through Stockbridge like wildfire and panic seized many in the town, causing them to flee south to what they hoped would be safer havens than Stockbridge.

Over the following weeks Stockbridge became an armed camp. The Edwards home was fortified by a surrounding wall of stakes (a palisade) and a number of the children—Lucy, Elizabeth and Pierpont—sent to the safety of Northampton. In the early stages of the war things went badly for the British, but Edwards seemed unruffled and

expressed confidence in a British victory ultimately. In the autumn of 1755 Edwards was able to visit Esther and her husband in Newark for Princeton's commencement at which he preached. In August of the following year (1756), Esther, with her baby son Aaron, Jr., returned the favour and made the trek to Stockbridge. On what turned out to be her last visit with her family, she stayed for three weeks, from 30 August to 22 September.

Not far from Stockbridge Esther was caught in a thunderstorm and arrived soaked to the skin. Despite this and the fatigue from the journey she noted she 'could not sleep for fear of the enemy'. A few days later she noted that she was 'almost overcome with fear' because of the possibility of an attack on Stockbridge. She observed, 'O how distressing to live in fear

Above: Aaron Burr Jr.

Left: The gravestone of Aaron Burr Jr.(standing) at the foot of his father and grandfather in the Princeton Cemetery

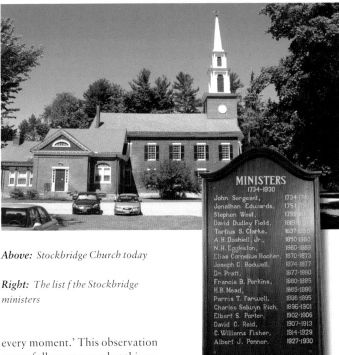

Above: Stockbridge Church today

Right: The list f the Stockbridge ministers

MINISTERS
1734-1930

John Sergeant,	1734-1749
Jonathan Edwards,	1751-1758
Stephen West,	1759-1818
David Dudley Field,	1819-1837
Tertius S. Clarke,	1837-1850
A. H. Dashiell, Jr.,	1850-1860
N. H. Eggleston,	1860-1869
Elias Cornelius Hooker,	1870-1873
Joseph C. Bodwell,	1874-1877
Dr. Pratt,	1877-1880
Francis B. Perkins,	1880-1885
H. B. Mead,	1885-1886
Parris T. Farwell,	1886-1895
Charles Selwyn Rich,	1896-1901
Elbert S. Porter,	1902-1906
David C. Reid,	1907-1913
C. Williams Fisher,	1914-1929
Albert J. Penner,	1927-1930

every moment.' This observation powerfully captures what things must have been like at the time for the Edwards household, though, as has been mentioned, her father was generally able to live above many of the fears that gripped others.

Esther had originally intended to stay until the second week of October. When her mother announced, a week after Esther's arrival, that she had to go to Northampton to help her younger sister Mary, who was about to deliver her third child, Esther decided to cut short her stay. Her fear of being 'butchered by a barbarous enemy', as she put it, only increased her desire to leave. Esther tried to reconcile herself to dying in such a manner if it were God's will and reminded herself that 'the Lord reigns' in all human affairs in this world. There were

times when this truth of God's sovereignty brought calm to her mind and heart, but at other times she was simply petrified.

It may well have been these petrifying fears that led to an extremely helpful discussion with her father on 18 September 1756. As she wrote in her Diary the following day:

'Last eve I had some free discourse with My Father on the great things that concern my best interest—I opened my difficulties to him very freely and he as freely advised and directed. The conversation has removed some distressing doubts that discouraged me much in my Christian warfare. He gave me some excellent directions to be observed in secret that tend to keep the soul near to God, as well as others to be observed in a more public way. What a mercy that I have such a Father! Such a Guide!'

Here is Edwards at his best: still the shepherd of his family. If the matter of trusting in God's sovereignty was the issue that led to this conversation, Edwards would have shown Esther how it was, in his words, a 'delightful conviction' and a doctrine that was 'sweet'. But the conversation also appears to have involved what we call spiritual disciplines and what Esther described as 'directions…to keep the soul near to God.' Esther left for home the following Wednesday afternoon and reached Newark nine days later.

Loving the Mahicans

Perhaps some of Esther's fears had to do with the fact that Edwards had located his home right among the Indians at Stockbridge, the first of the British settlers to do so. What this meant was that Edwards and his family had daily contact with the Indians. His son, Jonathan Edwards, Jr., would later recall how his earliest boyhood friends were Indian boys and that he was completely at home in speaking Mahican, a dialect of the Algonquian language that John Eliot had mastered in the previous century. In fact, the younger Edwards recalled, 'I knew the names of some things in Indian which I did not know in English.' The elder Edwards was unable to speak any of the Indian languages, but he deeply desired that his son learn to communicate with the Indians. In the spring of 1755, despite the war that was raging, he and Sarah allowed Jonathan Jr. to accompany the missionary Gideon Hawley on his mission to the Oneida settlement of Onohquaga, two hundred miles away!

Edwards genuinely loved the Indians as equals, in the words of Stephen Nichols: 'He showed remarkable sensitivity to Native Americans.' Among his writings that survive from this period is a statement of faith that he had drawn up for some of the Indian converts to confess before the Stockbridge church so that they might become full members of the church. It affirms

Above: *Although he comes after Edwards' time, Samson Occom had connections with the Stockbridge Indians and is historically the most famous native American to be associated with Eleazer Wheelock's Indian School (now Dartmouth College)*

a commitment to the 'one living and true God, who is the Father, the Son and the Holy Ghost' as the believer's 'highest and sweetest good'.

One of the Mahicans impacted by Edwards was Hendrick Aupaumut, who was born in 1757 and probably was baptized by Edwards before he left Stockbridge. Thirty years later Aupaumut wrote a letter to Edwards' son, Timothy, who as a merchant was still living in Stockbridge. Aupaumut was eager to get hold of copies of Edwards' *Religious Affections* and his *Freedom of the Will* (on which, see below). Aupaumut went on to translate the *Westminster Shorter Catechism* into Mahican and apparently left a significant spiritual legacy among his people.

'The Arminian controversy'

Edwards' confidence in divine sovereignty had been resolved many years before at the time

Top: A convert preaching to his fellow Indians

Above *Henrich Aupaumut was famous among the Mahican Indians and may have been baptised as an infant by Edwards in the year Edwards left Stockbridge*

of his conversion. 'Absolute sovereignty,' he later confessed, 'is what I love to ascribe to God.' But the doubts that he had had with regard to God's sovereignty, usually bound up with the theological system known as Calvinism, were increasingly common in 18th century New England. For those

Arminianism

Historically, classical Arminianism takes its name from Jacob Arminius (1560–1609), a Dutch theologian who maintained that divine predestination is conditional on a person's response to the gospel. This was contrary to the Calvinist conviction that Christ died for his elect people. Arminius argued that Christ's death was for every human being, though only believers would be saved. Seeking to preserve human freedom, Arminius further argued that God's saving grace can be resisted. Though the views of Arminius and his followers were condemned at the Synod of Dort (1618–1619), those views flourished in England during the late 17th century as well as taking on a rationalistic hue. A good illustration of this English embrace of Arminianism can be found in the writings of Henry More, a Cambridge theologian who died in 1687. More was a vigorous opponent of the Calvinistic doctrine of predestination and believed that it was 'to blaspheme reason ... to reproach Heaven itself and to dishonour the God of reason'. In 1686, the Calvinistic citadel of New England's Harvard College adopted a treatise on ethics written by More, and the entire theological orientation of the school began to shift towards 'a greater emphasis on man's natural reason, inherent dignity and inviolable freedom', as theologian Samuel T Logan has expressed it.

Left: A portrait of Timothy Cutler

who did not find their theological doubts silenced as Edwards had experienced, there was an increasingly attractive alternative in Arminianism.

The most spectacular case of Arminian thinking in the early years of Edwards' lifetime was the defection of Timothy Cutler, the Yale College Rector in 1722, see page 18. His defection involved both an embrace of Anglicanism and a wholesale rejection of the Calvinist worldview. In fact, by 1730 Edwards' brother-in-law James Pierpont could say that Yale had been 'corrupted and ruined with Arminianism and heresy'. This linkage of Arminianism and heresy is noteworthy. In the minds of men like Pierpont and his brother-in-law, Edwards, Calvinism was biblical Christianity and any deviation from it threatened men and women with spiritual loss. In the 1730s, to Edwards' great consternation, numerous younger ministers in New England were 'under prejudices against' Calvinism and 'argue for, propagate, and preach the Arminian scheme.'

Two classics of Calvinist theology

Although the Great Awakening in the 1740s brought about a renewed respect for Calvinism—all of the major leaders in it, apart from the Wesley brothers in England, were Calvinists—Edwards rightly believed that Arminianism was still a problem. So in that decade, Edwards began to read works for and against Calvinism in preparation for a definitive defence of Calvinism. Edwards might have been ready to begin writing in 1747, but then David Brainerd came to Northampton and subsequently died there, and

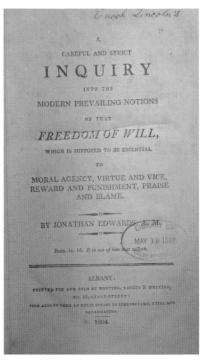

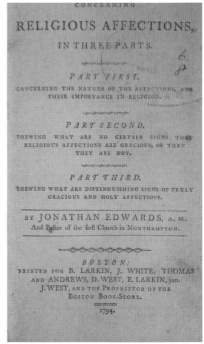

Top right: The title page of The Inquiry into the Freedom of the Will. *This was Edwards' reply to the Arminian controversy, completed after many hindrances*

Right: The title page of Religious Affections. *Completed in 1746 it was intended as a middle way between Chauncy's rationalism Davenport's excesses*

Edwards devoted 1748 to writing Brainerd's memoir.

It was not until July of 1752 that he informed his Scottish correspondent John Erskine that he hoped to have 'leisure to resume my design of writing something on the Arminian controversy'. As it turned out, he did not find the time until early the following year. It is obvious that Stockbridge was not a place of quiet retreat. Demands on his time as a pastor and missionary, coupled with the care of his family and the alarms of war, kept him from what had been long-term literary desires. However, on 14 April 1753 he happily informed Erskine, 'After many hindrances, delays and interruptions, divine providence has so favoured me, and smiled on my design of writing on the Arminian controversy, that I have almost finished the first draft.' It was completed that December and published the following year as *A Careful and Strict Enquiry into the Modern Prevailing Notions of That Freedom of Will, Which is Supposed to be Essential to Moral Agency*. It is usually known simply as *Freedom of the Will*.

The great aim of the book was to show from Scripture that human responsibility can be held at the same time as the assertion that God orders absolutely everything that happens in the universe. Ultimately what was critical for Edwards was upholding the unqualified sovereignty of God. If the sovereignty of God forms the boundaries within which the Christian theologian must reason,

what type of human freedom is then conceivable? Contrary to the Arminian assertion that genuine moral freedom must mean liberty from all constraint, Edwards argued that human beings are free only insofar as they do what their nature and wills desire, and as such they can be held responsible for their moral choices.

The other great work of theology that emerged from the Stockbridge years was Edwards' *The Great Christian Doctrine of Original Sin Defended* (1758), which was a defence of the doctrine long held in Augustinian and Reformed circles that our sinful actions are the result of our sinfulness, which is rooted in our solidarity with Adam. Adam's fall into sin imprinted on all of his progeny an 'innate sinful depravity of the heart'. Edwards knew that to assert anything less about the human condition outside of Christ was to endanger the biblical doctrine of justification by faith alone and grace alone. This doctrine only makes sense in the light of the fact that human beings are ultimately utterly helpless to change their hearts to will what was good. The radical depravity of the human heart and the glory of God's sovereign grace in salvation are so inextricably interwoven that one cannot confess the latter without holding fast to the former.

The call to Princeton—and home
Much of the writing of these two books, and others during the Stockbridge years, was on paper scrounged from every

possible source—old bills, pamphlets no longer needed, and the backs of letters. This is indicative of the financial straits in which he and his family found themselves during these years. In fact, at the beginning of 1752 Edwards told his father that he was £2,000 pounds in debt. Despite these financial woes and the ever-present dangers from the war, when, in September 1757, Edwards was offered the Presidency of the College of New Jersey, which had recently moved to Princeton, he was extremely reluctant to leave the frontier.

His son-in-law, Aaron Burr, Sr., had died unexpectedly from a fever on 24 September, and five days later the trustees of the college had written to Edwards, asking him to consider the Presidency. Edwards replied on 19 October in the negative. He was conscious of various physical weaknesses and a temperament marked 'by a disagreeable dullness and stiffness' that rendered him a

Above: Nassau Hall, Princeton University, formerly the New College of New Jersey, was built by the bequest of New Jersey Governor Jonathan Belcher and named after King William III of the House of Nassau. It was complete before Edwards' arrival. Only the exterior is original, the interior having been gutted by more than one fire

poor conversationalist. As he said, 'I can write better than I can speak.' He also had certain gaps in his learning—the higher parts of mathematics and the Greek classics, for example. In addition there were various literary projects in which he was engaged that he did not wish to put aside. But the request was not easily refused. A council of ministers, which included his close friend, Samuel Hopkins, met the following January and recommended that Edwards should accept the offer. Finally, Edwards made the journey to

Princeton in late January 1758, with plans to move the rest of the family there in early summer.

The new President preached in Nassau Hall every Lord's Day and gave some theological questions for the senior class to ponder and study. He also found time to spend with the children of his daughter Esther, his grandchildren Sally, then four and able to recite from memory some of the poetry that Isaac Watts had written for children, and Aaron, Jr., the future Vice-President, then but two years old and already quite a handful for his mother.

Edwards had been at the College only a few weeks when he was inoculated against smallpox, a great killer in the 18th century and which was raging in Princeton and the vicinity. The vaccine initially appeared to be successful, but complications set in. Edwards, as we have seen, had never been a strong man physically, and he died on 22 March 1758.

Among his last words were some for his wife, who was still at Stockbridge with most of their children. To his two children who were present at his bedside, Esther and Lucy, he said a little before his death: 'Give my kindest love to my dear wife, and tell her, that the uncommon union, which has so long subsisted between us, has been of such a nature, as I trust is spiritual, and therefore will continue forever.' Just before his death, those at his bedside, supposing he was unconscious, were lamenting what his death would mean to the college and to the church, when they were surprised by what proved to be his last words: 'Trust in God, and

Right: This grave in the Presidents Plot of Princeton Cemetery contains the remains of Jonathan Edwards and his beloved Sarah who died that same year, 1758, in October. The inscription is in Latin and declares, among other things, that Edwards was 'an eminent Theologian with scarcely an equal ...A strong and invincible defender of the Christian faith' and one who was 'eminent for piety'. It ended by urging the reader to 'Follow his pious steps'

ye need not fear.' To the end Edwards maintained a God-centred focus: the living God was all-sufficient and would ever care for his church and for his family.

When Sarah received the news of Jonathan's death, she consoled herself and Esther in a short note: 'A holy and good God has covered us with a dark cloud. Oh that we may kiss the rod, and lay our hands over our mouths! The Lord has done it. He has made me adore his goodness, that we had him so long. But my God lives; and he has my heart.' In fact, the dark cloud would remain. Little did Sarah know when she penned this remarkable confession that her daughter Esther had also been taken ill and died. Determined to raise Esther's two children, Sally and Aaron Jr., Sarah travelled to Philadelphia and Princeton in September. Sadly she fell victim to dysentery and passed away on 2 October 1758. The God who had her heart in life now possessed her soul in glory. Her body was laid to rest beside Jonathan's in the Presidents Plot of Princeton Cemetery.

Edwards' legacy

When his wife Sarah heard of the death of her husband, she wrote to her daughter Esther, 'O what a legacy my husband, and your father, has left us!' What was that legacy?

A recent history of philosophy in America from the early 18th century to the present day, by Bruce Kuklick, begins with the significant contribution that

Top: The Presidents Plot in the Princeton Cemetery. Many famous Presidents and Professors are buried here including Edwards, Charles Hodge, Archibald Alexander, Joseph A Alexander, James W Alexander, Samuel Davies and John Witherspoon

Above: John Witherspoon, President of Princeton University from 1768 to 1794, was the only clergyman and college president to sign the Declaration of Independence

The legacy of missions: The Humble Attempt (1748)

Jonathan Edwards' involvement in the Northampton revival of 1734–1735 and the Great Awakening of 1740–1742 left him with the keen conviction that prayer for times of spiritual awakening, which would lead to the advance of Christ's kingdom in history, was central to seeing them take place. Thus he drew up and published in 1748 a treatise that sought to encourage believers to gather together regularly to pray for the pouring out of God's Spirit. It bore a typical 18th century title: *An Humble Attempt to Promote Explicit Agreement and Visible Union of God's People in Extraordinary Prayer, For the Revival of Religion and the Advancement of Christ's Kingdom on Earth, pursuant to Scripture-Promises and Prophecies concerning the Last Time.*

This treatise would have some impact during Edwards' own lifetime, but its main influence came during the final decades of the 18th century. In 1784 John Erskine, Edwards' one-time Scottish correspondent, sent a copy of this treatise to a young Baptist leader by the name of John Ryland, Jr. He, in turn, shared it with two close friends— Andrew Fuller and John Sutcliff. The result was the start of a prayer movement that was instrumental in the kindling of a significant revival

among the Baptists of Great Britain and the initiation of the modern missionary movement in which William Carey, a close friend of the three Baptists just named, played a prominent role. (See the Day One Travel Guide in this series *Travel with William Carey*) by Paul Pease.

Above: Title Page to Edwards' book, better known as The Humble Attempt

Edwards made to that history. His ideas and philosophical reflections dominated the studies of both philosophers and theologians down to the 1870s. Little wonder that Yale University Press, since the late 1950s, has been publishing his collected works. He is arguably America's greatest philosopher and theologian.

Edwards' life also speaks of faithfulness to the word of God. During the revivals that came to New England in his lifetime, there was much blessing, yet also much confusion about what truly was the work of the Spirit. Edwards turned to Scripture as the pre-eminent authority for determining what was genuine spirituality. Moreover, in an age when numerous intellectuals and authors were exalting human reason, Edwards was committed to divine revelation as the bedrock of truth.

At the beginning of his life, Calvinism was an embattled worldview and in decline. Through his writings, Edwards was the key individual in the 18th century who restored it to a place of spiritual vigour and influence. His writings have been a source of Calvinist renewal ever since.

Finally, Edwards' rich and profound collection of treatises, books, sermons, notes, and letters are filled with a God-exalting, Christ-centred focus. Modern-day evangelicalism, shaped more by pragmatism than the glory and beauty of the triune God, urgently needs to reflect on the theological perspective found in this body of writings.

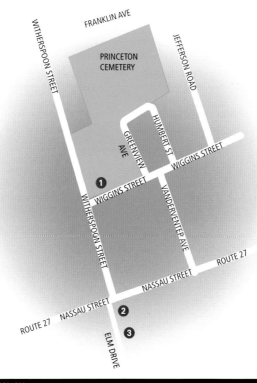

PRINCETON, NJ

1 PRINCETON CEMETERY: PRESIDENT'S PLOT ENTRANCE OFF GREENVIEW AVE
2 MACLEAN HOUSE, PRINCETON
UNIVERSITY
3 NASSAU HALL, PRINCETON, UNIVERSITY

Princeton University, Princeton, New Jersey 08544. ☎ 609–258–3000.

The Maclean House (built 1756) and Nassau Hall (initially constructed in 1756) of Princeton University, Princeton, NJ, were both present during Edwards' short tenure here as President. While Nassau Hall has suffered from both fire and other troubles, the Maclean House has been restored to its original condition. Built as the President's House it is the home in which Edwards died. There is a portrait of both Jonathan and Sarah Edwards housed here. For information, location and access to these two facilities one should contact the University directly.

Both Jonathan and Sarah Edwards are buried in the Princeton Cemetery, President's Plot which is not on the campus. The entrance is on Greenview Ave. In addition to Jonathan and Sarah, this cemetery has a number of significant people buried here including Aaron Burr Jr., Vice President of the U.S. and grandson to Jonathan and Sarah through the daughter Esther Edwards Burr and her husband Aaron Burr Sr. previous president of the seminary to Jonathan, Archibald Alexander, etc. A map of the cemetery can be procured on the cemetery website.

Above: *The Maclean House of Princeton University was the President's House during Edwards' day. His daughter, Esther and son-in-law Aaron Burr, Sr., would have lived here, as did Edwards for the short time he was president of the school. He would have suffered his final illness with daughters Esther and Lucy and the two Burr grandchildren in this house*

Summary of Edwards' life

Date	Event
5 October 1703	Jonathan Edwards born at East Windsor, Connecticut
29 February 1704	The Deerfield Massacre
9 January 1710	Sarah Pierpont born at New Haven, Connecticut
Before 1715	Sarah Pierpont's conversion
1716–1720	Edwards at Yale
1720	Receives Baccalaureate degree
Late spring 1721	Jonathan Edwards' conversion
October 1726	Begins preaching in Northampton
15 February 1727	Ordained at Northampton as assistant minister to Solomon Stoddard
28 July 1727	Marries Sarah Pierpont in New Haven
11 February 1729	Solomon Stoddard dies; Edwards becomes senior pastor
1734–1735	Northampton revival
1737	*Faithful Narrative* published in London
1738	Preaches the sermon series *Charity and Its Fruits* (published 1852)
1740	Great Awakening in New England begins
17–19 October 1740	George Whitefield preaches in Northampton
December 1740	Writes *Personal Narrative*
8 July 1741	Preaches *Sinners in the Hands of an Angry God* at Enfield, Connecticut
January–February 1742	Sarah Edwards has extraordinary experiences
March 1743	*Some Thoughts Concerning the present Revival of Religion in New-England* published
1746	Publishes *Religious Affections*
9 October 1747	David Brainerd dies in Edwards' home
October 1747	*Humble Attempt* published
Autumn 1748	Begins work on *An Account of the Life Of the late Reverend Mr. David Brainerd*
14 February 1748	Daughter Jerusha dies
December 1748	Completes *An Account of the Life Of the late Reverend Mr. David Brainerd*
1748–1750	Controversy between Edwards and his church
22 June 1750	Dismissed as pastor of Northampton
1 July 1750	Preaches Farewell Sermon
8 August 1751	Installed as pastor at Stockbridge
16 August 1751	Preaches to the Mohawks at Albany, New York
December 1754	*Freedom of the Will* published
May 1757	*The Great Christian Doctrine of Original Sin defended* finished
29 September 1757	Offered the presidency of the College of New Jersey
16 February 1758	Assumes the presidency of the College of New Jersey
23 February 1758	Inoculated for smallpox
22 March 1758	Dies of complications from the inoculation
7 April 1758	Daughter Esther Edwards Burr dies
2 October 1758	Sarah Edwards dies of dysentery in Philadelphia
1758	*Original Sin* published

THE RESOLUTIONS of Jonathan Edwards (the dates are in the form Edwards himself penned them). He began these in New York in 1722 at the age of 19.

Being sensible that I am unable to do anything without God's help, I do humbly entreat him by his grace to enable me to keep these resolutions, so far as they are agreeable to his will, for Christ's sake.

Remember to read over these Resolutions once a week.

1. Resolved, that I will do whatsoever I think to be most to God's glory, and my own good, profit and pleasure, in the whole of my duration, without any consideration of the time, whether now, or never so many myriads of ages hence. Resolved to do whatever I think to be my duty and most for the good and advantage of mankind in general. Resolved to do this, whatever difficulties I meet with, how many soever, and how great soever.

2. Resolved, to be continually endeavoring to find out some new contrivance and invention to promote the aforementioned things.

3. Resolved, if ever I shall fall and grow dull, so as to neglect to keep any part of these Resolutions, to repent of all I can remember, when I come to myself again.

4. Resolved, never to do any manner of thing, whether in soul or body, less or more, but what tends to the glory of God; nor be, nor suffer it, if I can avoid it.

5. Resolved, never to lose one moment of time; but improve it the most profitable way I possibly can.

6. Resolved, to live with all my might, while I do live.

7. Resolved, never to do anything, which I should be afraid to do, if it were the last hour of my life.

8. Resolved, to act, in all respects, both speaking and doing, as if nobody had been so vile as I, and as if I had committed the same sins, or had the same infirmities or failings as others; and that I will let the knowledge of their failings promote nothing but shame in myself, and prove only an occasion of my confessing my own sins and misery to God. **July 30.**

9. Resolved, to think much on all occasions of my own dying, and of the common circumstances which attend death.

10. Resolved, when I feel pain, to think of the pains of martyrdom, and of hell.

11. Resolved, when I think of any theorem in divinity to be solved, immediately to do what I can towards solving it, if circumstances do not hinder.

12. Resolved, if I take delight in it as a gratification of pride, or vanity, or on any such account, immediately to throw it by.

13. Resolved, to be endeavoring to find out fit objects of charity and liberality.

14. Resolved, never to do any thing out of revenge.

15. Resolved, never to suffer the least motions of anger towards irrational beings.

16. Resolved, never to speak evil of anyone, so that it shall tend to his dishonor, more or less, upon

no account except for some real good.

17. Resolved, that I will live so, as I shall wish I had done when I come to die.

18. Resolved, to live so, at all times, as I think is best in my devout frames, and when I have clearest notions of things of the gospel, and another world.

19. Resolved, never to do any thing, which I should be afraid to do, if I expected it would not be above an hour, before I should hear the last trump.

20. Resolved, to maintain the strictest temperance, in eating and drinking.

21. Resolved, never to do any thing, which if I should see in another, I should count a just occasion to despise him for, or to think any way the more meanly of him. (Resolutions 1 through 21 written in one setting in New Haven in 1722)

22. Resolved, to endeavor to obtain for myself as much happiness, in the other world, as I possibly can, with all the power, might, vigor, and vehemence, yea violence, I am capable of, or can bring myself to exert, in any way that can be thought of.

23. Resolved, frequently to take some deliberate action, which seems most unlikely to be done, for the glory of God, and trace it back to the original intention, designs and ends of it; and if I find it not to be for God's glory, to repute it as a breach of the 4th Resolution.

24. Resolved, whenever I do any conspicuously evil action, to trace it back, till I come to the original cause; and then, both

carefully endeavor to do so no more, and to fight and pray with all my might against the original of it.

25. Resolved, to examine carefully, and constantly, what that one thing in me is, which causes me in the least to doubt of the love of God; and to direct all my forces against it.

26. Resolved, to cast away such things, as I find do abate my assurance.

27. Resolved, never willfully to omit any thing, except the omission be for the glory of God; and frequently to examine my omissions.

28. Resolved, to study the Scriptures so steadily, constantly and frequently, as that I may find, and plainly perceive myself to grow in the knowledge of the same.

29. Resolved, never to count that a prayer, nor to let that pass as a prayer, nor that as a petition of a prayer, which is so made, that I cannot hope that God will answer it; nor that as a confession, which I cannot hope God will accept.

30. Resolved, to strive to my utmost every week to be brought higher in religion, and to a higher exercise of grace, than I was the week before.

31. Resolved, never to say any thing at all against any body, but when it is perfectly agreeable to the highest degree of Christian honor, and of love to mankind, agreeable to the lowest humility, and sense of my own faults and failings, and agreeable to the golden rule; often, when I have said anything against anyone, to

bring it to, and try it strictly by the test of this Resolution.

32. Resolved, to be strictly and firmly faithful to my trust, that, in Proverbs 20:6, 'A faithful man who can find?' may not be partly fulfilled in me.

33. Resolved, to do always, what I can towards making, maintaining, and preserving peace, when it can be done without overbalancing detriment in other respects. **Dec. 26, 1722.**

34. Resolved, in narrations never to speak any thing but the pure and simple verity.

35. Resolved, whenever I so much question whether I have done my duty, as that my quiet and calm is thereby disturbed, to set it down, and also how the question was resolved. **Dec. 18, 1722.**

36. Resolved, never to speak evil of any, except I have some particular good call for it. **Dec. 19, 1722.**

37. Resolved, to inquire every night, as I am going to bed, wherein I have been negligent, what sin I have committed, and wherein I have denied myself; also at the end of every week, month and year. **Dec. 22 and 26, 1722.**

38. Resolved, never to speak anything that is ridiculous, sportive, or matter of laughter on the Lord' s day. Sabbath evening, **Dec. 23, 1722.**

39. Resolved, never to do any thing of which I so much question the lawfulness of, as that I intend, at the same time, to consider and examine afterwards, whether it be lawful or not; unless I as much question the lawfulness of the omission.

40. Resolved, to inquire every night, before I go to bed, whether I have acted in the best way I possibly could, with respect to eating and drinking. **Jan. 7, 1723.**

41. Resolved, to ask myself, at the end of every day, week, month and year, wherein I could possibly, in any respect, have done better. **Jan. 11, 1723.**

42. Resolved, frequently to renew the dedication of myself to God, which was made at my baptism; which I solemnly renewed, when I was received into the communion of the church; and which I have solemnly re-made this twelfth day of **January, 1722–23.**

43. Resolved, never, henceforward, till I die, to act as if I were any way my own, but entirely and altogether God's; agreeable to what is to be found in Saturday, **January 12, 1723.**

44. Resolved, that no other end but religion, shall have any influence at all on any of my actions; and that no action shall be, in the least circumstance, any otherwise than the religious end will carry it. **January 12, 1723.**

45. Resolved, never to allow any pleasure or grief, joy or sorrow, nor any affection at all, nor any degree of affection, nor any circumstance relating to it, but what helps religion. **Jan. 12 and 13, 1723.**

46. Resolved, never to allow the least measure of any fretting uneasiness at my father or mother. Resolved to suffer no effects of it, so much as in the least alteration of speech, or motion of my eye: and to be especially careful of it with respect to any of our family.

47. Resolved, to endeavor, to my utmost, to deny whatever is not most agreeable to a good, and universally sweet and benevolent, quiet, peaceable, contented and easy, compassionate and generous, humble and meek, submissive and obliging, diligent and industrious, charitable and even, patient, moderate, forgiving and sincere temper; and to do at all times, what such a temper would lead me to; and to examine strictly, at the end of every week, whether I have done so. Sabbath morning. **May 5, 1723.**

48. Resolved, constantly, with the utmost niceness and diligence, and the strictest scrutiny, to be looking into the state of my soul, that I may know whether I have truly an interest in Christ or not; that when I come to die, I may not have any negligence respecting this to repent of. **May 26, 1723.**

49. Resolved, that this never shall be, if I can help it.

50. Resolved, I will act so as I think I shall judge would have been best, and most prudent, when I come into the future world. **July 5, 1723.**

51. Resolved, that I will act so, in every respect, as I think I shall wish I had done, if I should at last be damned. **July 8, 1723.**

52. I frequently hear persons in old age, say how they would live, if they were to live their lives over again: Resolved, that I will live just so as I can think I shall wish I had done, supposing I live to old age. **July 8, 1723.**

53. Resolved, to improve every opportunity, when I am in the best and happiest frame of mind, to cast and venture my soul on the Lord Jesus Christ, to trust and confide in him, and consecrate myself wholly to him; that from this I may have assurance of my safety, knowing that I confide in my Redeemer. **July 8, 1723.**

54. Whenever I hear anything spoken in conversation of any person, if I think it would be praiseworthy in me, Resolved to endeavor to imitate it. **July 8, 1723.**

55. Resolved, to endeavor to my utmost to act as I can think I should do, if, I had already seen the happiness of heaven, and hell torments. **July 8, 1723.**

56. Resolved, never to give over, nor in the least to slacken, my fight with my corruptions, however unsuccessful I may be.

57. Resolved, when I fear misfortunes and adversities, to examine whether I have done my duty, and resolve to do it, and let the event be just as providence orders it. I will as far as I can, be concerned about nothing but my duty, and my sin. **June 9, and July 13 1723.**

58. Resolved, not only to refrain from an air of dislike, fretfulness, and anger in conversation, but to exhibit an air of love, cheerfulness and benignity. **May 27, and July 13, 1723.**

59. Resolved, when I am most conscious of provocations to ill nature and anger, that I will strive most to feel and act good-naturedly; yea, at such times, to manifest good nature, though I think that in other respects it would be disadvantageous, and so as would be imprudent at other times. **May 12, July 11, and July 13.**

60. Resolved, whenever my feelings begin to appear in the least out of order, when I am conscious of the least uneasiness within, or the least irregularity without, I will then subject myself to the strictest examination. **July 4, and 13, 1723.**

61. Resolved, that I will not give way to that listlessness which I find unbends and relaxes my mind from being fully and fixedly set on religion, whatever excuse I may have for it, that what my listlessness inclines me to do, is best to be done, etc. **May 21, and July 13, 1723.**

62. Resolved, never to do anything but duty, and then according to Ephesians 6:6–8, to do it willingly and cheerfully as unto the Lord, and not to man:‹knowing that whatever good thing any man doth, the same shall he receive of the Lord. **June 25 and July 13, 1723.**

63. On the supposition, that there never was to be but one individual in the world, at any one time, who was properly a complete Christian, in all respects of a right stamp, having Christianity always shining in its true luster, and appearing excellent and lovely, from whatever part and under whatever character viewed: Resolved, to act just as I would do, if I strove with all my might to be that one, who should live in my time. **January 14 and July 13, 1723.**

64. Resolved, when I find those groanings which cannot be uttered (Romans 8:26), of which the Apostle speaks, and those breakings of soul for the longing it hath, of which the Psalmist speaks, Psalm 119:20, that I will promote them to the utmost of my power, and that I will not be weary of earnestly endeavoring to vent my desires, nor of the repetitions of such earnestness. **July 23, and August 10, 1723.**

65. Resolved, very much to exercise myself in this, all my life long, viz. with the greatest openness, of which I am capable of, to declare my ways to God, and lay open my soul to him: all my sins, temptations, difficulties, sorrows, fears, hopes, desires, and every thing, and every circumstance; according to Dr. Manton's 27th Sermon on Psalm 119. **July 26, and Aug.10 1723.**

66. Resolved, that I will endeavor always to keep a benign aspect, and air of acting and speaking in all places, and in all companies, except it should so happen that duty requires otherwise.

67. Resolved, after afflictions, to inquire, what I am the better for them, what am I the better for them, and what I might have got by them.

68. Resolved, to confess frankly to myself all that which I find in myself, either infirmity or sin; and, if it be what concerns religion, also to confess the whole case to God, and implore needed help. **July 23, and August 10, 1723.**

69. Resolved, always to do that, which I shall wish I had done when I see others do it. **August 11, 1723.**

70. Let there be something of benevolence, in all that I speak. **August 17, 1723.**

Further reading

The number of books on Edwards is becoming huge. Those below will give the reader excellent biographies of Edwards as well as up-to-date collections of essays that discuss various aspects of Edwards' thought and ongoing legacy.

D.G. Hart, Sean Michael Lucas, and Stephen J. Nichols, eds., *The Legacy of Jonathan Edwards: American Religion and the Evangelical Tradition* (Grand Rapids: Baker, 2003).

George M. Marsden, *Jonathan Edwards: A Life* (New Haven, CT: Yale University Press, 2003).

Iain H. Murray, *Jonathan Edwards—A New Biography* (Edinburgh: The Banner of Truth Trust, 1987).

John Piper and Justin Taylor, eds., *A God Entranced Vision of All Things: The Legacy of Jonathan Edwards* (Crossway Books, 2004).

With regard to Edwards' own works, there is the Yale University Press 26-volume edition of his writings, *The Works of Jonathan Edwards* (1957–2008).

For a one-volume collection of representative writings by Edwards, see John E. Smith, Harry S. Stout, and Kenneth P. Minkema, eds., *A Jonathan Edwards Reader*, (New Haven, CT: Yale University Press, 1995).

The one key online site to study Edwards is http://edwards.yale.edu/.

Acknowledgements

The authors would like to thank Anita Baines for her help in drawing the maps.

All pictures are the copyright of Ron Baines and MZW Photography of Grafton, MA.

p 4 Portraits of Jonathan and Sarah Edwards - Courtesy of Princeton University; gift of Dr. J. Pennington Warter, Class of 1942, Maclean House Princeton

p 21 Replica of Jonathan Edwards' Desk, courtesy of First Church of Wethersfield, Wethersfield, Ct..

p 37 James Pierpont, courtesy of the Yale University Art Gallery Bequest of Allen Evarts Foster, B.A. 1906

p 39 Sarah Pierpont, Courtesy of Princeton University; gift of Dr. J. Pennington Warter, Class of 1942

p 44 Esther Edwards Burr, Yale University Art Gallery Bequest of Oliver Burr Jennings, B.A. 1917, in memory of Miss Annie Burr Jennings

p 45 Aaron Burr Jr., courtesy of the Library of Congress

p 55 Title page of Sermons on the Following Subjects courtesy of the Portland Public Library, Portland, Maine

p 69 Portrait of Charles Chauncy courtesy of the First Church, Boston

p 71 Title Page of Sinners in the Hands of an Angry God, courtesy of the Rare Books Division, The New York Public Library, Astor, Lenox and Tilden Foundations

p 73 View of Newburyport courtesy of Isaac Makashinyi

p 75 Picture of Old South

Meeting House Courtesy of Old South Presbyterian Church, Newburyport, Ma

p 108 Picture of Aaron Burr Jr., courtesy of the Library of Congress

p 113 Title Page of Freedom of the Will, courtesy of Colby College Special Collections, Waterville, Maine.

p 113 Title Page of Religious Affections, courtesy of Colby College Special Collections, Waterville, Maine.

The authors

Dr. Michael A. G. Haykin

is Professor of Church History and Biblical Spirituality at The Southern Baptist Theological Seminary in Louisville, Kentucky, and Director of the Andrew Fuller Center for Baptist Studies at The Southern Baptist Theological Seminary. He is also a Research Professor of the Irish Baptist College at Queen's University, Belfast, N. Ireland. He and his wife, Alison, and two children, Victoria and Nigel, live in Dundas, Ontario. They attend West Highland Baptist Church in Hamilton, Ontario.

And my acknowledgments:

Without the help and prayers of my dear wife, Alison, this book would not have been possible. I would also like to thank Steve Jones, who worked in the archives at The Southern Baptist Theological Seminary library, for work beyond the call of duty.

Ronald Baines was born in Western Massachusetts almost halfway between Northampton and Stockbridge. He has been in the pastoral ministry for over twenty years and is currently pastor of Grace Reformed Baptist Church, in Topsham, Maine and a PhD candidate at the University of Maine. He resides in Brunswick, Maine. He and his wife Joan, who is descended from Edwards' eldest daughter Sarah, have four children.

Above: Jonathan Edwards' church in Main Street, Northampton, 1838